BRITANNICA
Mathematics
in
Context

# Some of the Parts

# Britannica

ENCYCLOPÆDIA BRITANNICA EDUCATIONAL CORPORATION

*Mathematics in Context* is a comprehensive middle grades curriculum. It was developed in collaboration with the Wisconsin Center for Education Research, School of Education, University of Wisconsin–Madison and the Freudenthal Institute at the University of Utrecht, The Netherlands, with the support of National Science Foundation Grant No. 9054928.

 **National Science Foundation**
Opinions expressed are those of the authors
and not necessarily those of the Foundation

# The *Mathematics in Context* Development Team

*Mathematics in Context* is a comprehensive middle grades curriculum. The National Science Foundation funded the National Center for Research in Mathematical Sciences Education at the University of Wisconsin–Madison to develop and field-test the materials from 1991 through 1996. The Freudenthal Institute at the University of Utrecht in The Netherlands is the main subcontractor responsible for the development of the student and assessment materials.

The initial version of *Some of the Parts* was developed by Frans van Galen and Monica Wijers. It was adapted for use in American schools by Gail Burrill and Mary S. Spence.

## National Center for Research in Mathematical Sciences Education Staff

Thomas A. Romberg
*Director*

Joan Daniels Pedro
*Assistant to the Director*

Gail Burrill
*Coordinator*
*Field Test Materials*

Margaret R. Meyer
*Coordinator*
*Pilot Test Materials*

Mary Ann Fix
*Editorial Coordinator*

Sherian Foster
*Editorial Coordinator*

James A. Middleton
*Pilot Test Coordinator*

### Project Staff

Jonathan Brendefur
Laura J. Brinker
James Browne
Jack Burrill
Rose Byrd
Peter Christiansen
Barbara Clarke
Doug Clarke
Beth R. Cole

Fae Dremock
Jasmina Milinkovic
Margaret A. Pligge
Mary C. Shafer
Julia A. Shew
Aaron N. Simon
Marvin Smith
Stephanie Z. Smith
Mary S. Spence

## Freudenthal Institute Staff

Jan de Lange
*Director*

Els Feijs
*Coordinator*

Martin van Reeuwijk
*Coordinator*

### Project Staff

Mieke Abels
Nina Boswinkel
Frans van Galen
Koeno Gravemeijer
Marja van den Heuvel-Panhuizen
Jan Auke de Jong
Vincent Jonker
Ronald Keijzer

Martin Kindt
Jansie Niehaus
Nanda Querelle
Anton Roodhardt
Leen Streefland
Adri Treffers
Monica Wijers
Astrid de Wild

# Acknowledgments

Several school districts used and evaluated one or more versions of the materials: Ames Community School District, Ames, Iowa; Parkway School District, Chesterfield, Missouri; Stoughton Area School District, Stoughton, Wisconsin; Madison Metropolitan School District, Madison, Wisconsin; Milwaukee Public Schools, Milwaukee, Wisconsin; and Dodgeville School District, Dodgeville, Wisconsin. Two sites were involved in staff development as well as formative evaluation of materials: Culver City, California, and Memphis, Tennessee. Two sites were developed through partnership with Encyclopædia Britannica Educational Corporation: Miami, Florida, and Puerto Rico. University Partnerships were developed with mathematics educators who worked with preservice teachers to familiarize them with the curriculum and to obtain their advice on the curriculum materials. The materials were also used at several other schools throughout the United States.

We at Encyclopædia Britannica Educational Corporation extend our thanks to all who had a part in making this program a success. Some of the participants instrumental in the program's development are as follows:

**Jefferson Elementary**
*Santa Ana, California*
Lydia Romero-Cruz

**Jefferson Middle School**
*Madison, Wisconsin*
Jane A. Beebe
Catherine Buege
Linda Grimmer
John Grueneberg
Nancy Howard
Annette Porter
Stephen H. Sprague
Dan Takkunen
Michael J. Vena

**Jesus Sanabria Cruz School**
*Yabucoa, Puerto Rico*
Andreíta Santiago Serrano

**John Muir Elementary School**
*Madison, Wisconsin*
Julie D'Onofrio
Jane M. Allen-Jauch
Kent Wells

**Kegonsa Elementary**
*Stoughton, Wisconsin*
Mary Buchholz
Louisa Havlik
Joan Olsen
Dominic Weisse

**Linwood Howe Elementary**
*Culver City, California*
Sandra Checel
Ellen Thireos

**Mitchell Elementary**
*Ames, Iowa*
Henry Gray
Matt Ludwig

**New School of Northern Virginia**
*Fairfax, Virginia*
Denise Jones

**Northwood Elementary**
*Ames, Iowa*
Eleanor M. Thomas

**Orchard Ridge Elementary**
*Madison, Wisconsin*
Mary Paquette
Carrie Valentine

**Parkway West Middle School**
*Chesterfield, Missouri*
Elissa Aiken
Ann Brenner
Gail R. Smith

**Ridgeway Elementary**
*Ridgeway, Wisconsin*
Lois Powell
Florence M. Wasley

**Roosevelt Elementary**
*Ames, Iowa*
Linda A. Carver

**Roosevelt Middle**
*Milwaukee, Wisconsin*
Sandra Simmons

**Ross Elementary**
*Creve Coeur, Missouri*
Annette Isselhard
Sheldon B. Korklan
Victoria Linn
Kathy Stamer

**St. Joseph's School**
*Dodgeville, Wisconsin*
Rita Van Dyck
Sharon Wimer

**St. Maarten Academy**
*St. Peters, St. Maarten, NA*
Shareed Hussain

**Sarah Scott Middle School**
*Milwaukee, Wisconsin*
Kevin Haddon

**Sawyer Elementary**
*Ames, Iowa*
Karen Bush Hoiberg

**Sennett Middle School**
*Madison, Wisconsin*
Brenda Abitz
Lois Bell
Shawn M. Jacobs

**Sholes Middle School**
*Milwaukee, Wisconsin*
Chris Gardner
Ken Haddon

**Stephens Elementary**
*Madison, Wisconsin*
Katherine Hogan
Shirley M. Steinbach
Kathleen H. Vegter

**Stoughton Middle School**
*Stoughton, Wisconsin*
Sally Bertelson
Polly Goepfert
Jacqueline M. Harris
Penny Vodak

**Toki Middle School**
*Madison, Wisconsin*
Gail J. Anderson
Vicky Grice
Mary M. Ihlenfeldt
Steve Jernegan
Jim Leidel
Theresa Loehr
Maryann Stephenson
Barbara Takkunen
Carol Welsch

**Trowbridge Elementary**
*Milwaukee, Wisconsin*
Jacqueline A. Nowak

**W. R. Thomas Middle School**
*Miami, Florida*
Michael Paloger

**Wooddale Elementary Middle School**
*Memphis, Tennessee*
Velma Quinn Hodges
Jacqueline Marie Hunt

**Yahara Elementary**
*Stoughton, Wisconsin*
Mary Bennett
Kevin Wright

## Site Coordinators

**Mary L. Delagardelle**—Ames Community Schools, Ames, Iowa

**Dr. Hector Hirigoyen**—Miami, Florida

**Audrey Jackson**—Parkway School District, Chesterfield, Missouri

**Jorge M. López**—Puerto Rico

**Susan Militello**—Memphis, Tennessee

**Carol Pudlin**—Culver City, California

## Reviewers and Consultants

**Michael N. Bleicher**
*Professor of Mathematics*
University of Wisconsin–Madison
Madison, WI

**Diane J. Briars**
*Mathematics Specialist*
Pittsburgh Public Schools
Pittsburgh, PA

**Donald Chambers**
*Director of Dissemination*
University of Wisconsin–Madison
Madison, WI

**Don W. Collins**
*Assistant Professor of Mathematics Education*
Western Kentucky University
Bowling Green, KY

**Joan Elder**
*Mathematics Consultant*
Los Angeles Unified School District
Los Angeles, CA

**Elizabeth Fennema**
*Professor of Curriculum and Instruction*
University of Wisconsin-Madison
Madison, WI

**Nancy N. Gates**
University of Memphis
Memphis, TN

**Jane Donnelly Gawronski**
*Superintendent*
Escondido Union High School
Escondido, CA

**M. Elizabeth Graue**
*Assistant Professor of Curriculum and Instruction*
University of Wisconsin–Madison
Madison, WI

**Jodean E. Grunow**
*Consultant*
Wisconsin Department of Public Instruction
Madison, WI

**John G. Harvey**
*Professor of Mathematics and Curriculum & Instruction*
University of Wisconsin–Madison
Madison, WI

**Simon Hellerstein**
*Professor of Mathematics*
University of Wisconsin–Madison
Madison, WI

**Elaine J. Hutchinson**
*Senior Lecturer*
University of Wisconsin–Stevens Point
Stevens Point, WI

**Richard A. Johnson**
*Professor of Statistics*
University of Wisconsin–Madison
Madison, WI

**James J. Kaput**
*Professor of Mathematics*
University of Massachusetts–Dartmouth
Dartmouth, MA

**Richard Lehrer**
*Professor of Educational Psychology*
University of Wisconsin–Madison
Madison, WI

**Richard Lesh**
*Professor of Mathematics*
University of Massachusetts–Dartmouth
Dartmouth, MA

**Mary M. Lindquist**
*Callaway Professor of Mathematics Education*
Columbus College
Columbus, GA

**Baudilio (Bob) Mora**
*Coordinator of Mathematics & Instructional Technology*
Carrollton-Farmers Branch Independent School District
Carrollton, TX

**Paul Trafton**
*Professor of Mathematics*
University of Northern Iowa
Cedar Falls, IA

**Norman L. Webb**
*Research Scientist*
University of Wisconsin–Madison
Madison, WI

**Paul H. Williams**
*Professor of Plant Pathology*
University of Wisconsin–Madison
Madison, WI

**Linda Dager Wilson**
*Assistant Professor*
University of Delaware
Newark, DE

**Robert L. Wilson**
*Professor of Mathematics*
University of Wisconsin–Madison
Madison, WI

## Dear Teacher,

Welcome! *Mathematics in Context* is designed to reflect the National Council of Teachers of Mathematics Standards for School Mathematics and to ground mathematical content in a variety of real-world contexts. Rather than relying on you to explain and demonstrate generalized definitions, rules, or algorithms, students investigate questions directly related to a particular context and construct mathematical understanding and meaning from that context.

The curriculum encompasses 10 units per grade level. This unit is designed to be the first in the number strand for grade 5/6, but it also lends itself to independent use—to introduce students to fractions, as well as to informal addition, subtraction, multiplication, and division calculations.

In addition to the Teacher Guide and Student Books, *Mathematics in Context* offers the following components that will inform and support your teaching:

• *Teacher Resource and Implementation Guide,* which provides an overview of the complete system, including program implementation, philosophy, and rationale

• *Number Tools,* which is a series of blackline masters that serve as review sheets or practice pages involving number issues and basic skills

• *News in Numbers,* which is a set of additional activities that can be inserted between or within other units; it includes a number of measurement problems that require estimation.

• *Teacher Preparation Videos,* which present comprehensive overviews of the units to help with lesson preparation

Thank you for choosing *Mathematics in Context.* We wish you success and inspiration!

Sincerely,

*The Mathematics in Context Development Team*

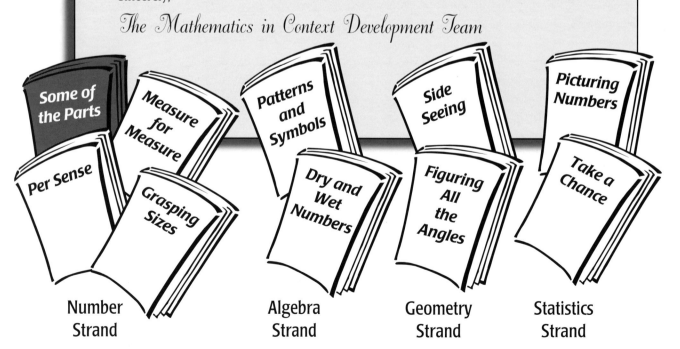

Number Strand    Algebra Strand    Geometry Strand    Statistics Strand

# Overview

BRITANNICA

Mathematics in Context

# How to Use This Book

This unit is one of 40 for the middle grades. Each unit can be used independently; however, the 40 units are designed to make up a complete, connected curriculum (10 units per grade level). There is a Student Book and a Teacher Guide for each unit.

Each Teacher Guide comprises elements that assist the teacher in the presentation of concepts and in understanding the general direction of the unit and the program as a whole. Becoming familiar with this structure will make using the units easier.

Each Teacher Guide consists of six basic parts:

- Overview
- Student Material and Teaching Notes
- Assessment Activities and Solutions
- Glossary
- Blackline Masters
- Try This! Solutions

## Overview

Before beginning this unit, read the Overview in order to understand the purpose of the unit and to develop strategies for facilitating instruction. The Overview provides helpful information about the unit's focus, pacing, goals, and assessment, as well as explanations about how the unit fits with the rest of the *Mathematics in Context* curriculum.

Note: After reading the Overview, view the Teacher Preparation Videotape that corresponds with the strand. The video models several activities from the strand.

## Student Materials and Teaching Notes

This Teacher Guide contains all of the student pages (except the Try This! activities), each of which faces a page of solutions, samples of students' work, and hints and comments about how to facilitate instruction. Note: Solutions for the Try This! activities can be found at the back of the Teacher Guide.

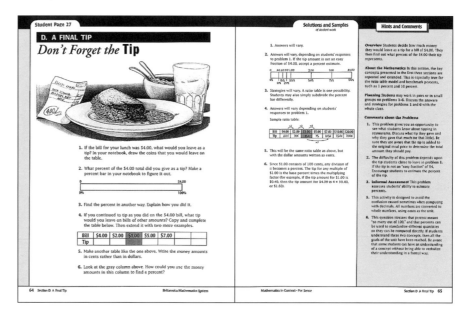

Each section within the unit begins with a two-page spread that describes the work students do, the goals of the section, new vocabulary, and materials needed, as well as providing information about the mathematics in the section and ideas for pacing, planning instruction, homework, and assessment.

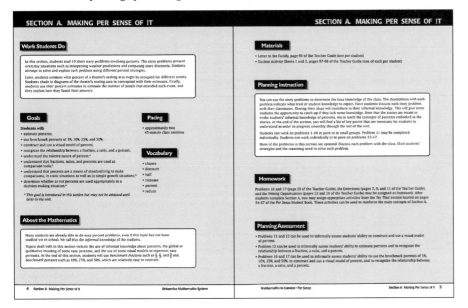

# Assessment Activities and Solutions

Information about assessment can be found in several places in this Teacher Guide. General information about assessment is given in the Overview; informal assessment opportunities are identified on the teacher pages that face each student page; and the Assessment Activities section of this guide provides formal assessment opportunities.

# Glossary

The Glossary defines all vocabulary words listed on the Section Opener pages. It includes mathematical terms that may be new to students, as well as words associated with the contexts introduced in the unit. (Note: The Student Book does not have a glossary. This allows students to construct their own definitions, based on their personal experiences with the unit activities.)

# Blackline Masters

At the back of this Teacher Guide are blackline masters for photocopying. The blackline masters include a letter to families (to be sent home with students before beginning the unit), several student activity sheets, and assessment masters.

# Try This! Solutions

Also included in the back of this Teacher Guide are the solutions to several Try This! activities—one related to each section of the unit—that can be used to reinforce the unit's main concepts. The Try This! activities are located in the back of the Student Book.

# Unit Focus

This unit focuses on operations with fractions. It begins by reviewing and extending basic notions about fractions and relationships between them through contexts involving food and cooking. Students estimate how much of a sandwich each person in a group will receive by dividing rectangular representations of submarine sandwiches. These rectangles are used to introduce a model for the part-whole relationship: the fraction bar. The ratio table is introduced within the context of recipes. Students use a ratio table to change amounts of ingredients as serving sizes change. The unit continues with an introduction to operations with fractions. Students add, subtract, multiply, and divide fractions using very informal methods. Students are expected to use their number sense related to fractions to solve problems in a variety of contexts.

All aspects of fractions appear in this unit, but no formal calculation methods are introduced. Throughout the unit, students are encouraged to use informal strategies to solve problems in which fractions are involved.

# Mathematical Content

- understanding that a fraction is the result of a division
- understanding that a fraction is a description of a part-whole relationship
- using fractions as measures
- building constructions from side and top views
- understanding fraction as numbers
- using mixed numbers
- understanding the equivalency of fractions
- estimating with fractions
- understanding the relative nature of fractions
- using operations with fractions

# Prior Knowledge

This unit assumes that students have:

- an understanding and recognition of benchmark fractions, such as $\frac{1}{2}, \frac{1}{3}, \frac{2}{3}, \frac{1}{4}, \frac{3}{4}$, and so on and,
- experience with dividing rectangles into equal pieces.

The unit may take less than three weeks when done after activities using the number line and ratio table from *Number Tools*.

Facility with adding and subtracting with up to three-digit numbers and with multiplying and dividing two-digit numbers is helpful for this unit. Students should also be able to read tables, use a number to perform estimations, and read a map.

Students who have already studied the unit *Patterns and Symbols* will have experience with repeated division by two (halving) and with multiplication by two (doubling).

This unit should be taught before the units *Measure for Measure, Per Sense,* and *Grasping Sizes.*

# Planning and Preparation

## Pacing: 14–15 days

| Section | Work Students Do | Pacing* | Materials |
|---|---|---|---|
| **A.** Sharing Food | ■ explore part-whole relationships<br>■ use benchmark fractions<br>■ use equivalent benchmark fractions in a context | 2 days | ■ Letter to the Family (one per student)<br>■ Student Activity Sheets 1–3 (one of each per student)<br>■ transparencies of Student Activity Sheets 1 and 3, optional, (one of each per class)<br>■ extra copies of Student Activity Sheet 2, optional (15 per class)<br>■ fruit tapes and/or submarine sandwiches, optional (one per group or class)<br>■ scissors (one pair per student)<br>■ glue or tape (one bottle or roll per pair or group of students)<br>■ rulers, optional (one per student) |
| **B.** Measure Up | ■ use fractions as measures of quantities<br>■ explore fractional relationships<br>■ find equivalent fractions<br>■ use mixed numbers<br>■ informally add fractions<br>■ explore the relative nature of fractions | 3–4 days | ■ Student Activity Sheets 4 and 5 (one of each per student)<br>■ tin cans or other containers (six per pair or group of students)<br>■ fraction strips (one set per student)<br>■ paper strips or string, optional (four per pair of students)<br>■ scissors (one pair per student)<br>■ magic markers, optional (one set per class)<br>■ See page 19 of the Teacher Guide for a list of optional materials and quantities needed |
| **C.** Fractions and Recipes | ■ add, subtract, multiply, and informally divide fractions, using a ratio table<br>■ explore constant relationships<br>■ use metric measurements for volume | 3 days | ■ Student Activity Sheets 6–8 (one of each per student)<br>■ set of standard measuring cups, fraction strips, one-liter measuring cup, additional recipes, all optional (see page 37 for quantities needed) |
| **D.** How Much? | ■ divide a whole into equal parts<br>■ use fractions as estimates for parts of a whole<br>■ use fraction relationships | 3 days | ■ Student Activity Sheets 9 and 10 (one of each per student)<br>■ cereal or other food boxes (several per class)<br>■ population data from class, school, or town<br>■ See page 55 of the Teacher Guide for a list of optional materials and quantities needed |
| **E.** How Far? | ■ understand multiplication of fractions as repeated addition<br>■ use fractions as operators<br>■ use equivalent forms of fractions | 3 days | ■ Student Activity Sheets 11 and 12 (one of each per student)<br>■ string or yarn (about one foot per student)<br>■ rulers, optional (one per student)<br>■ transparency of map on p. 32 of Student Book, optional (one per class)<br>■ paper strips, optional (two per student) |

\* One day is approximately equivalent to one 45-minute class session.

# Preparation

In the *Teacher Resource and Implementation Guide* is an extensive description of the philosophy underlying both the content and the pedagogy of the *Mathematics in Context* curriculum. Suggestions for preparation are also given in the Hints and Comments columns of this Teacher Guide. You may want to consider the following:

- Work through the unit before teaching it. If possible, take on the role of the student and discuss your strategies with other teachers.
- Use the overhead projector for student demonstrations, particularly with overhead transparencies of the student activity sheets and any manipulatives used in the unit.
- Invite students to use drawings and examples to illustrate and clarify their answers.
- Allow students to work at different levels of sophistication. Some students may need concrete materials, while others can work at a more abstract level.
- Provide opportunities and support for students to share their strategies, which often differ. This allows students to take part in class discussions and introduces them to alternative ways to think about the mathematics in the unit.
- In some cases, it may be necessary to read the problems to students or to pair students to facilitate their understanding of the printed materials.
- A list of the materials needed for this unit is in the chart on page xiii.
- Try to follow the recommended pacing chart on page xiii. You can easily spend more time on this unit than the number of class periods indicated. Bear in mind, however, that many of the topics introduced in this unit will be revisited and covered more thoroughly in other *Mathematics in Context* units.

# Resources

| For Teachers | For Students |
|---|---|
| **Books and Magazines** *Mathematics Assessment: Myths, Models, Good Questions, and Practical Suggestions,* edited by Jean Kerr Stenmark (Reston, Virginia: The National Council of Teachers of Mathematics, Inc., 1991) | **Videos** MathSense Video • *How Fractions Work* (available from Encyclopædia Britannica) |
| **Videos** *Number Strand Teacher Preparation Video* | |

# Assessment

## Planning Assessment

In keeping with the NCTM Assessment Standards, valid assessment should be based on evidence drawn from several sources. (See the full discussion of assessment philosophies in the *Teacher Resource and Implementation Guide*.) An assessment plan for this unit may draw from the following sources:

- Observations—look, listen, and record observable behavior.

- Interactive Responses—in a teacher-facilitated situation, note how students respond, clarify, revise, and extend their thinking.

- Products—look for the quality of thought evident in student projects, test answers, worksheet solutions, or writings.

These categories are not meant to be mutually exclusive. In fact, observation is a key part of assessing interactive responses and also key to understanding the end results of projects and writings.

## Ongoing Assessment Opportunities

- **Problems within Sections**
  To evaluate ongoing progress, *Mathematics in Context* identifies informal assessment opportunities and the goals that these particular problems assess throughout the Teacher Guide. There are also indications as to what you might expect from your students.

- **Section Summary Questions**
  The summary questions at the end of each section are vehicles for informal assessment (see Teacher Guide pages 16, 34, 52, 70, and 86).

## End-of-Unit Assessment Opportunities

In the back of this Teacher Guide are five problems that, when combined, form an end-of-unit assessment that will occupy one class session. For a more detailed description of these assessment activities, see the Assessment Overview (Teacher Guide pages 88 and 89).

You may also wish to design your own culminating project or let students create one that will tell you what they consider important in the unit. For more assessment ideas, refer to the charts on pages xvi and xvii.

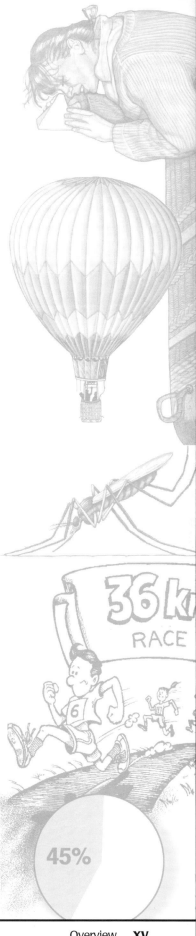

78%

## Goals and Assessment

In the *Mathematics in Context* curriculum, unit goals, categorized according to cognitive procedures, relate to the strand goals and the NCTM Curriculum and Evaluation Standards. Additional information about these goals is found in the *Teacher Resource and Implementation Guide.* The *Mathematics in Context* curriculum is designed to help students develop their abilities so that they can perform with understanding in each of the categories listed below. It is important to note that the attainment of goals in one category is not a prerequisite to attaining those in another category. In fact, students should progress simultaneously toward several goals in different categories.

| | Goal | Ongoing Assessment Opportunities | End-of-Unit Assessment Opportunities |
|---|---|---|---|
| **Conceptual and Procedural Knowledge** | **1.** recognize part-whole relationships | **Section A** p. 8, #4<br>**Section C** p. 50, #14b | Remember When? p. 115<br>Bars of Different Sizes, p. 116 |
| | **2.** use fractions to describe part-whole relationships | **Section A** p. 8, #4<br>**Section B** p. 30, #13<br>**Section D** p. 66, #8, #9 | Remember When? p. 115<br>Bars of Different Sizes, p. 116 |
| | **3.** estimate fractions and parts of wholes | **Section B** p. 34, #19<br>**Section D** p. 60, #3<br>p. 62, #4<br>p. 70, #13 | A Cycling Race, p. 118 |

| | Goal | Ongoing Assessment Opportunities | | End-of-Unit Assessment Opportunities |
|---|---|---|---|---|
| Reasoning, Communicating, Thinking, and Making Connections | 4. use informal strategies for operations with fractions | Section B | p. 28, #8–#10 p. 30, #13 | Bars of Different Sizes, p. 116 Tropical Smoothie, p. 117 A New Fence, p. 119 |
| | | Section C | p. 46, #8 p. 52, #18 | |
| | | Section E | p. 82, #11 p. 84, #14, #15 | |
| | 5. use equivalent forms of benchmark fractions within a context | Section A | p. 12, #7, #8 p. 16, #10b | Tropical Smoothie, p. 117 A Cycling Race, p. 118 |
| | | Section C | p. 48, #13 | |
| | | Section E | p. 82, #12 | |
| | 6. order and compare fractions within a context | Section E | p. 82, #12 | Remember When? p. 115 Bars of Different Sizes, p. 116 A Cycling Race, p. 118 |
| | 7. develop an understanding of and use the relationships between benchmark fractions | Section A | p. 12, #7, #8 p. 16, #10b | Remember When? p. 115 Tropical Smoothie, p. 117 A Cycling Race, p. 118 |
| | | Section B | p. 30, #13 p. 34, #18 | |
| | | Section C | p. 46, #8 | |

| | Goal | Ongoing Assessment Opportunities | | End-of-Unit Assessment Opportunities |
|---|---|---|---|---|
| Modeling, Nonroutine Problem-Solving, Critically Analyzing, and Generalizing | 8. understand the relative nature of fractions | Section B | p. 32, #16 p. 34, #19 | Bars of Different Sizes, p. 116 A Cycling Race, p. 118 |
| | 9. solve contextual problems in which simple fractions are involved, using informal strategies | Section B | p. 34, #19 | Bars of Different Sizes, p. 116 Tropical Smoothie, p. 117 A Cycling Race, p. 118 A New Fence, p. 119 |
| | | Section C | p. 52, #18 | |
| | | Section D | p. 66, #8, #9 p. 70, #12 | |
| | | Section E | p. 86, #19, #20 | |

# More about Assessment

## Scoring and Analyzing Assessment Responses

Students may respond to assessment questions with various levels of mathematical sophistication and elaboration. Each student's response should be considered for the mathematics that it shows, and not judged on whether or not it includes an expected response. Responses to some of the assessment questions may be viewed as either correct or incorrect, but many answers will need flexible judgment by the teacher. Descriptive judgments related to specific goals and partial credit often provide more helpful feedback than percentage scores.

Openly communicate your expectations to all students, and report achievement and progress for each student relative to those expectations. When scoring students' responses try to think about how they are progressing toward the goals of the unit and the strand.

## Student Portfolios

Generally, a portfolio is a collection of student-selected pieces that is representative of a student's work. A portfolio may include evaluative comments by you or by the student. See the *Teacher Resource and Implementation Guide* for more ideas on portfolio focus and use.

A comprehensive discussion about the contents, management, and evaluation of portfolios can be found in *Mathematics Assessment: Myths, Models, Good Questions, and Practical Suggestions*, pp. 35–48.

## Student Self-Evaluation

Self-evaluation encourages students to reflect on their progress in learning mathematical concepts, their developing abilities to use mathematics, and their dispositions toward mathematics. The following examples illustrate ways to incorporate student self-evaluations as one component of your assessment plan.

- Ask students to comment, in writing, on each piece they have chosen for their portfolios and on the progress they see in the pieces overall.

- Give a writing assignment entitled "What I Know Now about [a math concept] and What I Think about It." This will give you information about each student's disposition toward mathematics as well as his or her knowledge.

- Interview individuals or small groups to elicit what they have learned, what they think is important, and why.

Suggestions for self-inventories can be found in *Mathematics Assessment: Myths, Models, Good Questions, and Practical Suggestions*, pp. 55–58.

## Summary Discussion

Discuss specific lessons and activities in the unit—what the student learned from them and what the activities have in common. This can be done in whole-class discussions, small groups, or in personal interviews.

# Connections across the *Mathematics in Context* Curriculum

*Some of the Parts* is the first unit in the number strand. The map below shows the complete *Mathematics in Context* curriculum for grade 5/6. It shows where the unit fits in the number strand, and where it fits in the overall picture.

A detailed description of the units, the strands, and the connections in the *Mathematics in Context* curriculum can be found in the *Teacher Resource and Implementation Guide*.

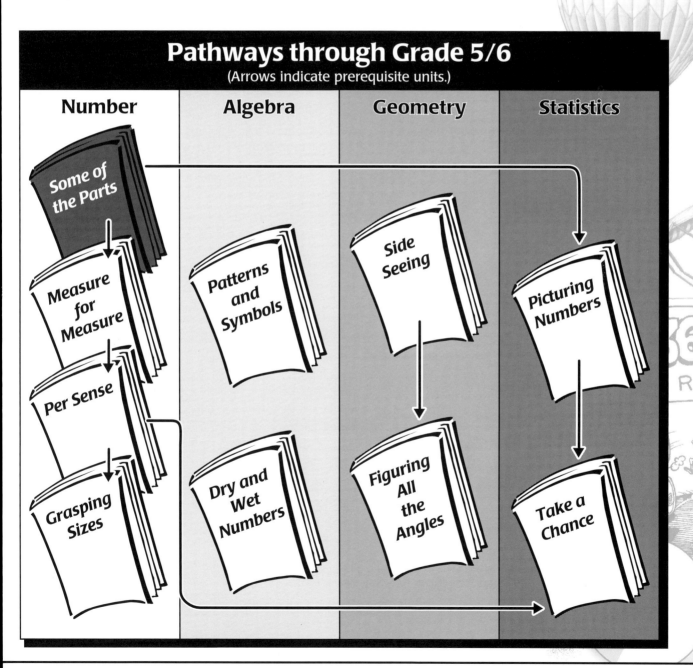

## Pathways through Grade 5/6
(Arrows indicate prerequisite units.)

| Number | Algebra | Geometry | Statistics |
|---|---|---|---|

- Some of the Parts
- Measure for Measure
- Per Sense
- Grasping Sizes
- Patterns and Symbols
- Dry and Wet Numbers
- Side Seeing
- Figuring All the Angles
- Picturing Numbers
- Take a Chance

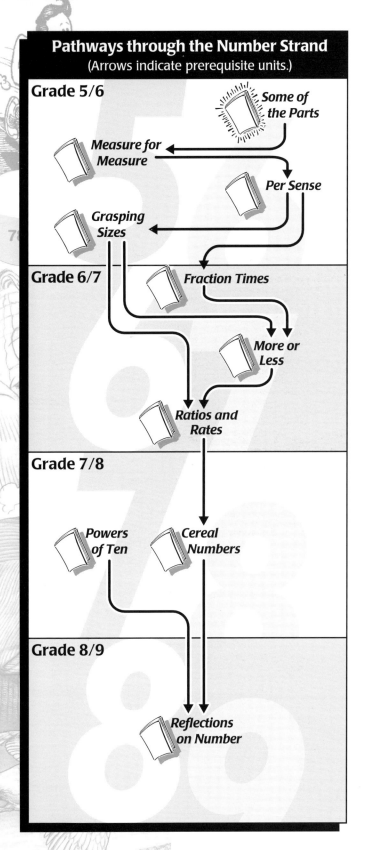

**Pathways through the Number Strand**
(Arrows indicate prerequisite units.)

Grade 5/6 — Some of the Parts, Measure for Measure, Per Sense, Grasping Sizes

Grade 6/7 — Fraction Times, More or Less, Ratios and Rates

Grade 7/8 — Powers of Ten, Cereal Numbers

Grade 8/9 — Reflections on Number

# Connections within the Number Strand

On the left is a map of the number strand; this unit, *Some of the Parts,* is highlighted.

*Some of the Parts* is the first unit in the number strand. A central feature of number concepts in all four grades is the development of several models that build and extend students' number sense. In this unit, two models are introduced and developed: the fraction bar and the ratio table. The development of these models is extended in the units *Measure for Measure, Per Sense,* and *Grasping Sizes.*

In *Some of the Parts,* operations with fractions are informally introduced, but student mastery is not expected. Students will revisit operations with fractions in more depth in *Fraction Times.*

The measurement problems are precursors to those in the unit *Measure for Measure.* Paper-folding activities and the ratio table are used in *Grasping Sizes* and *Ratios and Rates* to further develop the concept of ratio.

# The Number Strand

## Grade 5/6

### Some of the Parts
Using fractions to describe the relative magnitude of quantities; ordering fractions; and understanding performing addition, subtraction, and multiplication, and division operations with fractions.

### Measure for Measure
Representing and using decimals in a variety of equivalent forms, investigating relationships among fractions and decimals, extending decimal number sense, and adding and subtracting decimals.

### Per Sense
Understanding percents as representing part-whole relationships; understanding the relationship between fractions, percents, and ratios; and developing strategies for estimating and calculating percents.

### Grasping Sizes
Developing a conceptual sense of ratio, estimating and calculating the effects of proportional enlargements or reductions, using scale lines, organizing data into ratio tables and calculating ratios, and writing fractions as alternative expressions for equivalence situations.

## Grade 7/8

### Cereal Numbers
Measuring volume and surface area in metric units; noting how changes in volume affect changes in the surface area of rectangular prisms; making comparisons with ratios, fractions, decimals, and percents; using a visual model to multiply with fractions; and using a ratio strategy to divide with fractions.

### Powers of Ten
Investigating simple laws for calculating with powers of 10, and investigating very large and very small numbers.

## Grade 6/7

### Fraction Times
Comparing, adding, subtracting, and multiplying fractions and understanding the relationship among fractions, percents, decimals, and ratios.

### More or Less
Connecting fractions, decimals, and percents; exploring percents as operators; and discovering the effects of decimal multiplication.

### Ratios and Rates
Relating ratios to fractions, decimals, and percents; dividing with decimals; differentiating between part-part and part-whole ratios; and understanding the notions of rate, scale factor, and ratio as linear functions.

## Grade 8/9

### Reflections on Number
Exploring primes, prime factorization, and divisibility rules; analyzing algorithms for multiplication and division; and discovering and relating whole numbers, integers, and rational and irrational numbers by looking at the results of basic operations with their inverses.

## Connections with Other *Mathematics in Context* Units

The activities that involve doubling and halving ingredients for recipes will help students make connections with the algebra units *Patterns and Symbols* and *Ups and Downs*. In the statistics units *Picturing Numbers* and *Dealing with Data*, fractions are used to express distributions and to describe data.

Fractions also appear throughout the *Mathematics in Context* curriculum. Since most problem situations deal with real and rational numbers, students should be able to understand, interpret, and be able to use these numbers. In the geometry strand, fractions are used to express ratios and tangents.

The following mathematical topics included in the unit *Some of the Parts* are introduced or further developed in other *Mathematics in Context* units.

## Topics Revisited in Other Units

| Topic | Unit | Grade |
|---|---|---|
| number line, ratio table | *Number Tools* | |
| fractions, decimals | *Measure for Measure* | 5/6 |
| fractions, percents | *Per Sense* | 5/6 |
| fractions, ratios | *Grasping Sizes* | 5/6 |
| | *Ratios and Rates* | 6/7 |
| | *Looking at an Angle\*\*\** | 7/8 |
| fractions, decimals, percents | *More or Less* | 6/7 |
| | *Fraction Times* | 6/7 |
| | *Looking at an Angle\*\*\** | 7/8 |
| operations with fractions | *Fraction Times* | 6/7 |
| | *Cereal Numbers* | 7/8 |
| repeated halving/doubling | *Patterns and Symbols\*\** | 5/6 |
| | *Ups and Downs\*\** | 7/8 |
| | *Growth\*\** | 8/9 |
| metric measurement | *Measure for Measure* | 5/6 |
| | *Ratios and Rates* | 6/7 |
| | *More or Less* | 6/7 |
| fractions/decimals/division | *Picturing Numbers\** | 5/6 |
| | *Dealing with Data\** | 6/7 |
| | *Tracking Graphs\*\** | 6/7 |

  \* These units in the statistics strand also help students make connections to ideas about numbers.
 \*\* These units in the algebra strand also help students make connections to ideas about numbers.
\*\*\* These units in the geometry strand also help students make connections to ideas about numbers.

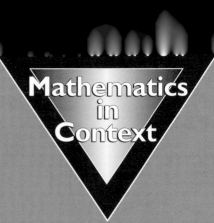

Mathematics
in
Context

# Student Materials and Teaching Notes

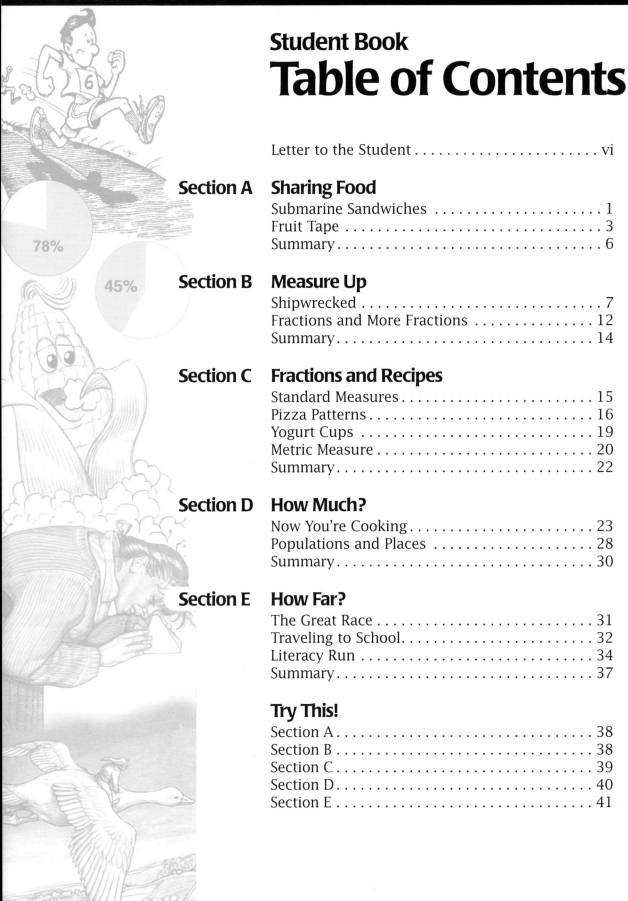

## Student Book
# Table of Contents

**Britannica Mathematics System**

# Dear Student,

Welcome to *Some of the Parts.*

In this unit, you will learn how the parts of quantities and objects we call fractions relate to the whole.

You will use fractions to measure and combine quantities of milk. Will $\frac{1}{3}$ of a can of milk and $\frac{5}{8}$ of a can of milk fit into one can?

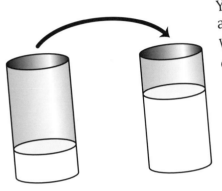

Knowing about relationships between fractions will help you alter recipes to serve different numbers of people.

You will also learn how fractions can help you measure and calculate distances.

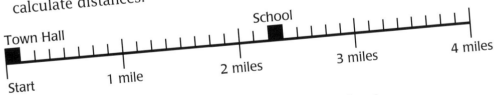

In the end, you should understand something about relationships between fractions. You will also use your understanding of fractions to add, subtract, multiply, and divide with them.

Sincerely,

*The Mathematics in Context Development Team*

# SECTION A. SHARING FOOD

## Work Students Do

Students study the part-whole relationships of fractions within the context of dividing submarine sandwiches equally among different-sized groups. They divide rectangular representations of sandwiches to determine the portion that each student in a group will receive. Students may invent various strategies for dividing the sandwiches. They then formalize the part-whole relationships by writing the fraction of a sandwich that each person will receive. Students are also introduced to *fraction strips* known as fruit tapes. Fruit tapes are rectangular strips of paper that are divided into equal-sized parts to represent halves, thirds, fourths, and so on. Students use these fraction strips throughout the unit to perform operations with fractions.

## Goals

**Students will:**

- recognize part-whole relationships;
- use fractions to describe part-whole relationships;
- use equivalent forms of benchmark fractions within a context;
- develop an understanding of and use the relationships between benchmark fractions.

## Pacing

- approximately two 45-minute class sessions

## Vocabulary

- fraction
- fraction strips
- part-whole relationship

## About the Mathematics

In this unit, students investigate the *part-whole relationships* of fractions and explore the concept of dividing a whole into equal parts. They also discover how simple fractions are related to each other. Students' real-life experiences in dividing a whole into equal parts should help them to relate the formal fraction notation to their informal understanding of part-whole relationships. Students use both words and fractions to describe partitioned submarine sandwiches, such as *two times $\frac{1}{3}$ of a sub* or *half of $\frac{1}{4}$ of a sub*. Concrete activities, such as making drawings and folding fruit tapes to show how to divide wholes into equal parts, also aid students in understanding part-whole relationships and the relationships between simple fractions. Fractions with the numerator one—such as $\frac{1}{2}$, $\frac{1}{4}$, and $\frac{1}{8}$—are the focus of this section.

## Materials

- Letter to the Family, page 102 of the Teacher Guide (one per student)
- Student Activity Sheets 1–3, pages 103–105 of the Teacher Guide (one of each per student)
- fruit tapes and/or submarine sandwiches, page 5 of the Teacher Guide, optional (one per group or class)
- transparency of Student Activity Sheet 1, page 9 of the Teacher Guide, optional (one per class)
- extra copies of Student Activity Sheet 2, page 11 of the Teacher Guide, optional (15 per class)
- scissors, page 11 of the Teacher Guide (one pair per student)
- glue or tape, page 11 of the Teacher Guide (one bottle or roll per pair or group of students)
- transparency of Student Activity Sheet 3, page 13 of the Teacher Guide, optional (one per class)
- rulers, page 15 of the Teacher Guide, optional (one per student)

## Planning Instruction

You might want to introduce this unit with a short discussion about the context of this section: dividing submarine sandwiches and fruit tapes to create equal shares. If possible, have fruit tapes or sub sandwiches on hand. Ask students such questions as: *How would you divide one fruit tape so that two students each get an equal amount? four students get an equal amount? five students get an equal amount?* [For two students, divide the fruit tape into two equal halves; for four students, divide the tape into fourths; for five students, divide the tape into fifths.]

Students may work individually on problems 1 and 2 and then share their answers with a partner or small group. Students may work on problems 3 and 5–10 individually or in pairs.

There are no optional problems in this section.

## Homework

Problem 4 (page 8 of the Teacher Guide) and problem 10 (page 16 of the Teacher Guide) can be assigned as homework. The Writing Opportunities (pages 7 and 17 of the Teacher Guide) and the Extensions (pages 13 and 15 of the Teacher Guide) may also be assigned as homework. After students complete Section A, you may assign appropriate activities from the Try This! section located on pages 38–41 of the *Some of the Parts* Student Book. The Try This! activities reinforce the key math concepts introduced in this section.

## Planning Assessment

- Problem 4 can be used to informally assess students' ability to recognize part-whole relationships and use fractions to describe part-whole relationships.
- Problems 7, 8, and 10b can be used to informally assess students' understanding of and ability to use the relationships between benchmark fractions and to use equivalent forms of benchmark fractions within a context.

# SUBMARINE *Sandwiches*

At Booker T. Washington Middle School, a class is planning a nature hike. The class is divided into groups of students. Each group of students pools their money to buy submarine sandwiches for lunch. When lunchtime arrives, each group shares the subs *equally.*

Above, you see four groups and the number of subs they have to share.

**1.** In which group do the students get the most to eat? Explain your answer.

**2.** In which group do the students get the least to eat? Explain your answer.

1. The students in Group D get the most to eat. Explanations will vary. Sample explanations:

   • Groups A, B, and D each have three subs. Since Group D has only two students, they will have more to eat than those in Groups A and B. When you compare Groups D and C, you see that Group C has more students than Group D but less food. This means that the students in Group D will have the most to eat.

   • Each student in Group D gets more than one whole sub, while the students in the other groups get less than one sub. This shows that the students in Group D get the most to eat.

   • Each student in Group A gets half a sub. Each student in Group D gets more than one whole sub. Each student in Groups B and C gets more than half a sub, but less than one whole sub. So, the students in Group D get the most to eat.

   Other possible explanations will be discussed in problem **3.**

2. The students in Group A get the least to eat. Explanations will vary. Sample student explanation:

   In problem 1, I found that the people in Group D had the most to eat, so I can eliminate Group D. Groups A and B have the same number of subs, but Group A has more people, so they have less to eat. So Group B can be eliminated. Then I compared Groups A and C. Group A is sharing three subs among six people, which is the same as sharing $1\frac{1}{2}$ subs among three people. Group C is sharing two subs among three people. Therefore, the people in Group A have the least to eat.

**Overview** Students investigate four situations in which different-sized groups of students want to equally divide a certain number of submarine sandwiches. Students determine in which groups a student gets the most and the least to eat.

**About the Mathematics** The problems on this page informally introduce students to the concept of fractions. Some students may use fractions explicitly to solve these problems. Others may simply compare the number of students to the number of submarine sandwiches in each group to divide the subs equally.

**Planning** You might introduce the context of this section with a brief discussion using one or more of the suggestions from the Planning Instruction section on page 5 of the Teacher Guide. Have students work individually on problems **1** and **2** and then share their solutions and strategies with a partner or small group. You may then summarize the different strategies used in these problems. Do not stress the use of fractions at this point. Fractions will be formally used in solving problem **3** on the next page.

**Comments about the Problems**

1. If students are having difficulty, suggest that they look for groups in which there are more subs than students or ask them to draw a picture showing how the submarine sandwiches could be divided equally among the students in each group. This activity helps prepare students for problem **3.**

2. If students are having difficulty with this problem, ask them to determine whether or not each student in the different groups gets more or less than one-half of a sub. After problem **3,** you may ask students to return to this problem and solve it completely.

**Writing Opportunity** Ask students to recall a family dinner or meal with friends in which various food items had to be shared equally among the people present. Have them write a short paragraph describing how many people were at the meal and how the various food items were equally shared.

**Emmy gets ... ?**

**3.** Use the rectangles beside each picture on **Student Activity Sheet 1** to show how the sandwiches should be cut so that each student in the group gets an equal share. Color the piece or pieces for Emmy, Jake, Sandra, and Walter. Then use *fractions* to describe how much each person will get.

**Jake gets ... ?**

**Sandra gets ... ?**

**4.** Draw two other pictures of students with submarine sandwiches. Choose your own numbers for students and sandwiches. Show how the sandwiches could be shared equally. Describe with fractions how much each student will get.

**Walter gets ... ?**

**3.** Answers will vary. Some possible solutions are:

**a.** Emmy gets $\frac{1}{2}$ sub

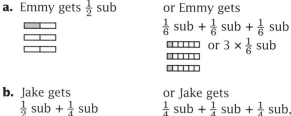

or Emmy gets

$\frac{1}{6}$ sub $+ \frac{1}{6}$ sub $+ \frac{1}{6}$ sub

or $3 \times \frac{1}{6}$ sub

**b.** Jake gets

$\frac{1}{2}$ sub $+ \frac{1}{4}$ sub

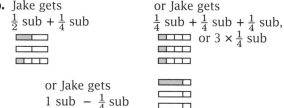

or Jake gets

$\frac{1}{4}$ sub $+ \frac{1}{4}$ sub $+ \frac{1}{4}$ sub,

or $3 \times \frac{1}{4}$ sub

or Jake gets

1 sub $- \frac{1}{4}$ sub

**c.** Sandra gets

$\frac{1}{3}$ sub $+ \frac{1}{3}$ sub,

or $2 \times \frac{1}{3}$ sub

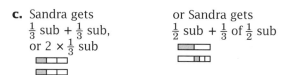

or Sandra gets

$\frac{1}{2}$ sub $+ \frac{1}{3}$ of $\frac{1}{2}$ sub

**d.** Walter gets

1 sub $+ \frac{1}{2}$ sub

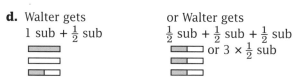

or Walter gets

$\frac{1}{2}$ sub $+ \frac{1}{2}$ sub $+ \frac{1}{2}$ sub

or $3 \times \frac{1}{2}$ sub

**4.** Answers will vary. Sample responses:

Easy solutions in which each child gets one whole sub:

2 people
2 subs

Each person gets one sub.

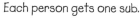

4 people
4 subs

Each person gets one sub.

More complex solutions in which fractions are used:

4 people
5 subs

Each person gets $1\frac{1}{4}$ subs.

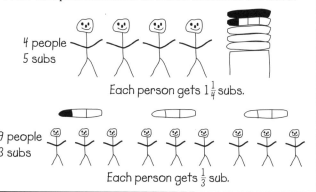

9 people
3 subs

Each person gets $\frac{1}{3}$ sub.

**Materials** Student Activity Sheet 1 (one per student); overhead transparency of Student Activity Sheet 1, optional (one per classroom)

**Overview** Students divide subs into equal parts for different-sized groups of students. They use a fraction to describe the portion that each person in each group receives. Students then write and solve their own problems within the same context of dividing subs.

**About the Mathematics** Students divide subs (rectangular drawings) into equal parts by drawing lines to indicate where each sub should be cut. Students' drawings may not show absolutely equal partitions. They may use combinations of words and fractions to describe their solutions.

**Planning** Have students work on problem **3** individually or in pairs. When discussing problem **3,** check to see whether different students' solutions are equivalent. This can be done visually by showing that the fractional parts drawn for different solutions are the same size. Make a transparency of Student Activity Sheet 1 if you want students to show their solutions on the overhead. Problem **4** can be assigned as homework and/or used as assessment.

**Comments about the Problems**

**3.** Some students may have difficulty correctly describing their solutions using fractions. Other students may forget to label each drawing with its correct fractional name. For example, in problem **3a,** some students may say that Emmy will receive $\frac{1}{2}$ of one sub, while others may answer that she will receive $\frac{1}{6}$ of all the subs. Both answers are correct if students understand what their fraction refers to. Stress that the first interpretation is the one that is meant here.

Some students may also neglect to take into account the relative sizes of the different sub parts. For example, in problem **3b,** they may count the parts they colored and determine that Jake gets two of the eight pieces, or $\frac{2}{8}$ of a sub. Jake does receive two pieces, but one piece is $\frac{1}{2}$ of a sub, and the other is $\frac{1}{4}$ of a sub.

**4. Informal Assessment** This problem assesses students' ability recognize part-whole relationships and use fractions to describe part-whole relationships. Student's drawings may show their level of understanding.

# FRUIT TAPE

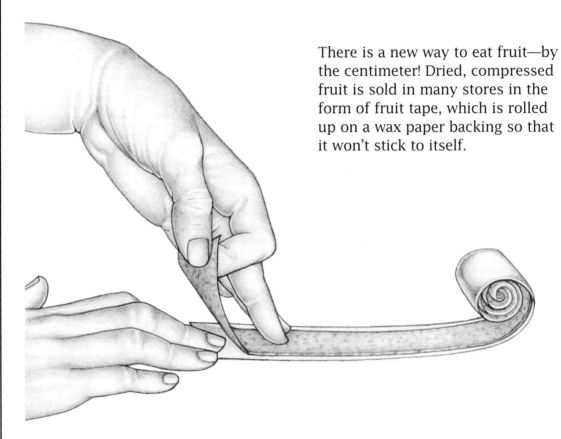

There is a new way to eat fruit—by the centimeter! Dried, compressed fruit is sold in many stores in the form of fruit tape, which is rolled up on a wax paper backing so that it won't stick to itself.

| 2 equal pieces | 4 equal pieces | 8 equal pieces | 3 equal pieces | 6 equal pieces | 5 equal pieces |
|---|---|---|---|---|---|
| | | | | | |

5. On **Student Activity Sheet 2,** you will find drawings of six pieces of fruit tape. Cut them out.

Divide and cut each fruit tape into the number of pieces indicated on **Student Activity Sheet 3.** Be sure that your pieces are equal. Glue the pieces onto the bars on **Student Activity Sheet 3.** Label each piece with a fraction. Be prepared to explain how you decided where to cut.

**5.**

| 2 equal pieces | 4 equal pieces | 8 equal pieces | 3 equal pieces | 6 equal pieces | 5 equal pieces |
|---|---|---|---|---|---|

Explanations will vary. Sample student explanation:

I folded a tape into three equal parts by first bending one end over the tape. Then I bent the other end over the top until it lined up with the first bend.

**Materials** Student Activity Sheets 2 and 3 (one of each per student); extra copies of Student Activity Sheet 2, optional (15 per classroom); scissors (one pair per student); glue or tape (one bottle or roll per pair or group of students)

**Overview** Students cut fruit tapes into equal parts and label each part with a fraction.

**About the Mathematics** Students make their own fraction fruit tapes to compare simple fractions by folding different strips of paper into so many equal parts. Encourage students to divide the tapes by folding, rather than by measuring. Measuring the tapes may divert their attention from the relationships between fractions, while folding the tapes stresses the idea of sharing equally and reinforces the fractional relationships involved. For example, in order to fold a tape into eight equal parts, the student must first fold the tape in half, then fold the tape in half two more times. This illustrates the relationships between the fractions $\frac{1}{2}$, $\frac{1}{4}$, and $\frac{1}{8}$. Fractions with a numerator other than one, such as $\frac{2}{5}$ or $\frac{3}{8}$ are not yet introduced. Students will learn about such fractions in Section B. The fraction tapes in this section can be used as a model during the rest of the unit.

**Planning** Students may work individually or in pairs on this problem. You may want to provide extra copies of Student Activity Sheet 2 for students who cut the strips incorrectly. All students should now understand how to label the parts of equally-divided tapes with fractions.

**Comments about the Problems**

**5.** Students may find it easier to cut the tapes into equal pieces if they first fold the tapes. If students are having difficulty folding their tapes into thirds or fifths, suggest the following strategies: *To fold a tape into three pieces, fold in one end of the strip and then fold the other end over until it lines up evenly with the first fold. To fold the tape into five sections, roll the tape until there are five equal sections and then press down to make the folds.*

**6.** Ten children want to share one fruit tape. Which fruit tape on **Student Activity Sheet 3** can you use to show how much each of them will get?

**7.** Two children want to share one fruit tape. Which tape can you use to show how much each will get? Are there several possibilities?

**8.** Three children want to share one fruit tape. Which tapes can you use to show how much each will get?

**6.** Answers will vary. Students may use any one of the fruit tapes to divide into equal pieces to be shared by the 10 students. If students subdivide the individual pieces of one fruit tape in half so that each of the 10 students receives an equal share, the following fruit tapes can be used:

The tape with five pieces can be used. Each of the five equal pieces can be divided into two equal pieces, for a total of 10 equal pieces.

The tape with two pieces can be used. Each of the two equal pieces can be divided into five equal pieces, for a total of 10 equal pieces.

**7.** Answers will vary. Students may use any one of the fruit tapes to divide into equal pieces to be shared by the two students. If students subdivide the individual pieces of one fruit tape in half so that each of the two students receives an equal share, the following fruit tapes can be used:

The tapes with two, four, six, or eight equal pieces can be used.

**8.** Answers will vary. Students may use any one of the fruit tapes to divide into equal pieces to be shared by the three students. If students subdivide the individual pieces of one fruit tape in thirds so that each of the three students receives an equal share, the following fruit tapes can be used:

The tapes with three or six equal pieces can be used.

**Materials** Student Activity Sheet 3 (one per student); transparency of Student Activity Sheet 3, optional (one per classroom)

**Overview** On this page, students use the fraction fruit tapes they just made to show how to divide one fruit tape equally among a certain number of students. Students explore the relationships between fractions with unlike denominators, such as halves, thirds, and sixths.

**About the Mathematics** Problems **6–8** help students begin to think about relationships between fractions with unlike denominators. Some students may use formal fractional computations such as $\frac{1}{2} \times \frac{1}{5} = \frac{1}{10}$ or $\frac{2}{6} = \frac{1}{3}$ to describe these relationships, while others may use words, such as *two-sixths is equal to one-third.*

**Planning** Students may work individually or in pairs on problems **6–8**. Encourage them to find all possible solutions for each problem.

**Comments about the Problems**

**6.** Encourage students to reuse one of the fruit tapes on Student Activity Sheet 3.

**7–8. Informal Assessment** These problems assess students' understanding of and their ability to use the relationships between benchmark fractions and to use equivalent forms of benchmark fractions within a context.

**Extension** You can ask students to create other problems similar to problems **7** and **8** to assess their ability to discover relationships between fractions. Also, if students understand problems **5–8,** you can ask them: *What can you do if seven children want to share a fruit tape?* [Divide the tape into seven equal parts.] You may then have students solve additional problems involving other numbers of students.

Edward was in a group of four. He got his equal share of one fruit tape. You can see it in his hand in the drawing below.

**9.** Draw a picture of the whole fruit tape. Explain how you figured out how long to make your drawing.

## Solutions and Samples
*of student work*

**9.** The whole fruit tape should be four times as long as the piece in Edward's hand. Student strategies for making the drawing may vary.

Sample strategies:

I marked off the length of the piece of fruit tape on a piece of paper four times.

I measured the length of the piece of fruit tape with a ruler. I multiplied that length by four and then drew a picture of the whole fruit tape.

## Hints and Comments

**Materials** ruler, optional (one per student)

**Overview** Given the size of one share of a fruit tape that was divided equally among four people, students determine the size of the whole fruit tape and then make a drawing of it.

**About the Mathematics** Students consider the inverse relationship between a part and a whole. On previous pages, students divided a whole into equal parts. Now they are given a part from which they must reconstruct the whole. Students also consider the relative nature of fractions.

**Planning** Students may work individually or in pairs on problem **9.** Have students discuss their strategies.

**Comments about the Problems**

**9.** Students should discover from the story that Edward's share is one-fourth of the whole fruit tape. Students' drawings do not have to be identical in size. Some may trace the piece as shown on the opposing Student Book page. In all cases, the whole should be drawn four times as large as the first piece.

You may want to ask students why their pictures of fourths are not the same size as the picture of fourths shown on Student Activity Sheet 3. This encourages students to think of the relative nature of fractions, an idea revisited on Student Book page 13.

**Extension** Ask students to create problems similar to problem **9.** Their problems can be used to assess students' understanding of part-whole relationships and of the relative nature of fractions. To challenge students, you may want to ask such questions as: *What would the size of the whole piece of fruit tape be if Edward were in a group of three instead of a group of four?* [The whole piece of fruit tape would be three times longer than his piece.]

# Summary

When you divide something into equal parts, you can name the parts with fractions.

This whole sub can be divided into three equal parts.

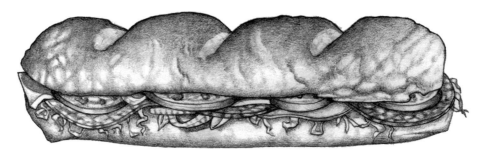

These parts can be called *thirds.* There are three parts. Each part is one-third of the whole.

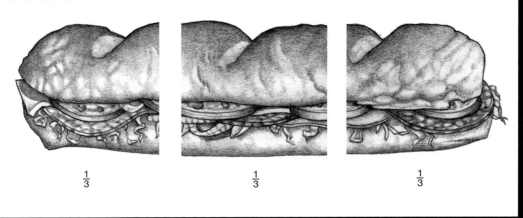

$\frac{1}{3}$ $\frac{1}{3}$ $\frac{1}{3}$

## Summary Questions

**10. a.** List some of the fractions you worked with in this section.

**b.** Describe how some of the fractions you listed might be related to each other.

## Solutions and Samples
*of student work*

**10. a.** Answers will vary. Possible student responses:

$\frac{1}{2}, \frac{1}{4}, \frac{1}{8}, \frac{1}{3}, \frac{1}{6}, \frac{1}{5}$, and $\frac{1}{10}$

**b.** Answers will vary. Possible relationships include:

Two times $\frac{1}{8}$ is $\frac{1}{4}$.

Half of $\frac{1}{4}$ is $\frac{1}{8}$.

Adding $\frac{1}{6}$ and $\frac{1}{6}$ and $\frac{1}{6}$ gives $\frac{1}{2}$.

One-half doubled is one whole.

One-fourth of $\frac{1}{2}$ is $\frac{1}{8}$.

One-tenth is half of $\frac{1}{5}$.

Three times $\frac{1}{3}$ is one whole.

## Hints and Comments

**Overview** Students read the Summary, which reviews the main concepts of this section. They then list some of the fractions used in Section A and describe the relationships between these fractions.

**Planning** Students may work individually or in pairs on problem **10.** You may decide to use this problem for assessment and/or homework. Be sure to discuss students' responses to problem **10b.** After students complete Section A, you may assign appropriate activities in the Try This! section, located on pages 38–41 of the Student Book, for homework.

**Comments about the Problems**

**10. a. Homework** This problem may be assigned as homework. Students may look back at earlier problems in Section A to list the fractions they used. All fractions should have the number one in the numerator. However, some students may have used fractions with a numerator other than one. These fractions are formerly introduced in Section B.

**10. b. Informal Assessment** This problem assesses students' understanding of and their ability to use the relationships between benchmark fractions and their ability to use equivalent forms of benchmark fractions within a context. Students may use their fraction tapes. They should use terms like *two times* or *double* or *together make* and *half of* when they describe relationships between the fractions. They may also use drawings. Do not require that students write their answers using formal notation, such as $\frac{1}{4} = \frac{1}{2} \times \frac{1}{2}$. Written answers, such as *one-fourth is one-half of one-half,* are equally as valid.

**Writing Opportunity** You may ask students to write letters to their parents in which they share and explain their answers for problem **10b.** This gives them the opportunity to clarify their understanding of the relationships between fractions. Encourage students to include drawings or sample problems in their letters.

# SECTION B. MEASURE UP

## Work Students Do

Students label and use measuring scales on tin cans of the same size in order to see the results of combining fractional quantities. They also fold fraction strips to show $\frac{3}{4}$ of a can, $\frac{5}{8}$ of a can, and so forth. Students then use fractions to estimate the amounts of coconut milk in different cans. They explore how to combine fractions with unlike denominators. Students also investigate addition with fractional quantities whose sums are one or less than one. The representation of fractional amounts on tin cans is replaced by fraction strips. The fraction strips are used to express relationships, such as $\frac{1}{3}$ can $+ \frac{1}{2}$ can $= \frac{5}{6}$ can. Finally, students are introduced to fractional quantities greater than one, such as $1\frac{1}{4}$ or $\frac{5}{4}$.

## Goals

**Students will:**

- use fractions to describe part-whole relationships;
- recognize part-whole relationships;*
- use informal strategies for operations with fractions;
- estimate fractions and parts of wholes;
- understand the relative nature of fractions;
- use equivalent forms of benchmark fractions within a context;*
- solve contextual problems in which simple fractions are involved, using informal strategies;
- develop an understanding of and use the relationships between benchmark fractions.

  *These goals are introduced in this section and assessed in later sections of the unit.*

## Pacing

- approximately three or four 45-minute class sessions

## Vocabulary

- denominator
- equivalent fraction
- improper fraction
- mixed number
- numerator

## About the Mathematics

The main concepts explored in this section include simple fractions, such as $\frac{3}{4}$, *mixed numbers,* such as $4\frac{1}{2}$, *improper fractions,* such as $\frac{10}{6}$, and *equivalent fractions,* such as $\frac{1}{4}$ and $\frac{2}{8}$. It is not important that students define and use these formal math terms at this point, since this unit serves as an informal introduction to fraction concepts. Students are also informally introduced to adding fractions and the relative nature of fractions. The problems, which ask students to combine fractional amounts in different cans into one can, are designed to build on students' understanding of benchmark fractions. Students do not need to know that when $\frac{1}{2}$ of a can of milk is poured into a can that is $\frac{3}{4}$ filled, the can will overflow. They can discover this by experimenting with real cans, by using the measuring scales on cans or fraction strips, or by reasoning with fractions. This section serves as an informal introduction to the concept of adding fractions with unlike denominators. No formal algorithm for adding fractions is discussed.

## Materials

- Student Activity Sheets 4–5, pages 106 and 107 of the Teacher Guide (one of each per student)
- transparency of Student Activity Sheet 5, page 31 of the Teacher Guide, optional (one per class)
- fraction strips from students' completed Student Activity Sheet 3, pages 23, 27, 29, 31, 33, and 35 of the Teacher Guide, optional (one set per student)
- tin can, page 23 of the Teacher Guide, optional (one per class)
- tin cans or plastic/glass cylinders of the same size, pages 25, 27, and 29 of the Teacher Guide (six per pair or group of students)
- paper strips or string, page 25 of the Teacher Guide, optional (four per pair of students)
- tape, page 25 of the Teacher Guide, optional (one roll per pair of students)
- wooden sticks, page 25 of the Teacher Guide, optional (one per pair of students)
- waterproof markers, page 25 of the Teacher Guide, optional  (one per pair of students)
- scissors, pages 25 and 31 of the Teacher Guide (one pair per student)
- magic markers, page 31 of the Teacher Guide, optional (one set per class)

## Planning Instruction

Section B is critical to this unit. You may want to introduce this section with a brief discussion of the shipwreck and the tin cans that washed ashore. The activity for problem 5, in which students mark measuring lines showing different fractional parts on cans, is important because it reinforces students' understanding of equivalent fractions. This activity may take half of one class session.

Students may work in pairs or in small groups on problems 8–11. They may work on the remaining problems individually or in pairs.

There are no optional problems in this section.

## Homework

Problems 4 (page 24 of the Teacher Guide), 9 and 10 (page 28 of the Teacher Guide), and 17–19 (page 34 of the Teacher Guide) can be assigned as homework. The Extensions (pages 23, 29, and 35 of the Teacher Guide) may also be assigned as homework. After students complete Section B, you may assign appropriate activities from the Try This! section located on pages 38–41 of the *Some of the Parts* Student Book. The Try This! activities reinforce the key math concepts introduced in this section.

## Planning Assessment

- Problems 8–10 can be used to informally assess students' ability to use informal strategies for operations with fractions.
- Problem 13 can be used to informally assess students' ability to use fractions to describe part-whole relationships and to use informal strategies for operations with fractions. It also assesses their understanding of and ability to use the relationships between benchmark fractions.
- Problem 16 can be used to informally assess students' understanding of the relative nature of fractions.
- Problem 18 can be used to informally assess students' understanding of and ability to use the relationships between benchmark fractions.
- Problem 19 may be used to informally assess students' understanding of the relative nature of fractions, as well as their ability to estimate fractions and parts of wholes and to solve contextual problems in which simple fractions are involved, using informal strategies.

## B. MEASURE UP

# Shipwrecked

You and a couple of friends are on a boat trip in the Pacific. Unfortunately, your boat hits a coral reef and begins to sink. You and your friends are able to swim to a nearby island.

When you explore the island, you discover that it offers a variety of food: coconut milk, all sorts of berries, and several kinds of fruit.

You are very lucky! Some tin cans have washed ashore. This makes the coconut milk easier to drink and allows you to share it when the coconut supply is low.

## Solutions and Samples
*of student work*

## Hints and Comments

**Overview** The story on this page introduces the context of Section B, in which students pretend that they are shipwrecked with friends on a deserted island. They find coconut milk to drink and tin cans that can be used to equally share it.

**About the Mathematics** Tin cans are used to measure liquids. Students will use fractions to describe the contents of the cans. Fractions with numerators other than one will also be introduced in this section.

**Planning** Read the story together as a class and have students discuss how the tin cans can be used for sharing the coconut milk.

**Interdisciplinary Connection** You may have interested students read related literature involving shipwrecks, such as *Robinson Crusoe* by Daniel Defoe. You may wish to discuss other appropriate book selections with a language arts or social studies teacher.

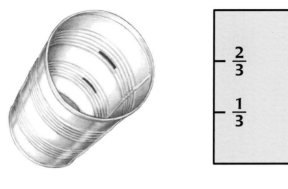

$$\frac{2}{3}$$

$$\frac{1}{3}$$

Sometimes you find that you want less than a whole can of coconut milk, so you scratch lines inside the cans as pictured on the left.

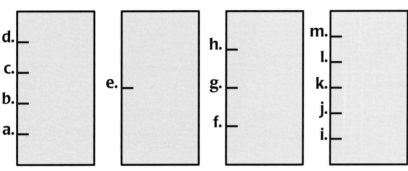

d.
c.
b.
a.

e.

h.
g.
f.

m.
l.
k.
j.
i.

**1.** In your notebook, write the fractions that you would put beside the measuring points labeled *a* through *m*.

In a fraction, the number written above the line segment is called the **numerator**.

The number written below the line segment is called the **denominator**.

$$\frac{2}{3} \begin{array}{l} \Leftarrow \textbf{\textit{numerator}} \\ \Leftarrow \textbf{\textit{denominator}} \end{array}$$

**2.** Explain what the numerator and denominator in a fraction mean.

**1. a.** $\frac{1}{5}$    **e.** $\frac{1}{2}$    **i.** $\frac{1}{6}$    **m.** $\frac{5}{6}$

   **b.** $\frac{2}{5}$    **f.** $\frac{1}{4}$    **j.** $\frac{2}{6}$

   **c.** $\frac{3}{5}$    **g.** $\frac{2}{4}$    **k.** $\frac{3}{6}$

   **d.** $\frac{4}{5}$    **h.** $\frac{3}{4}$    **l.** $\frac{4}{6}$

**2.** Answers will vary. Sample student responses:

The numerator is the number written above the line segment in a fraction. It tells you how many equal parts to shade. The denominator is the number written below the line segment in a fraction. It tells you how many equal parts you have in all.

The denominator represents the total number of equal parts into which the whole is divided. The numerator represents the number of equal parts that make up the portion of the whole. (It is the shaded part of the whole.)

**Materials** tin can, optional (one per classroom); fraction strips from students' completed Student Activity Sheet 3, optional (one per student).

**Overview** Students use fractions with numerators other than one to describe the level of coconut milk in a tin can.

**About the Mathematics** Fractions with a numerator greater than one are introduced here. In the fruit tape activity in Section A, each piece was labeled with a fraction with a numerator of one; here there are no individual pieces. Fractions are used to indicate what part of a whole can is filled with milk.

**Planning** After students read the text, discuss the meaning of the pictures and make sure that all students understand the use of the fractions $\frac{1}{3}$ and $\frac{2}{3}$. You may want to use a real can to clarify the story and the picture. If students do not understand the use of the fraction $\frac{2}{3}$, do part of problem **1** together. Students may work on these problems individually or in pairs. Discuss students' answers for both problems. At this point, all students should understand which fractions correspond with the various measuring points.

**Comments about the Problems**

**1.** If students are having difficulty, have them look at the fruit tapes from Student Activity Sheet 3 and ask them questions such as *What could $\frac{1}{3}$ and $\frac{1}{3}$ together be named?* [two $\frac{1}{3}$s or $\frac{2}{3}$] Suggest that they lengthen the lines for the measuring points in the rectangular models of the cans so that they look more like the fruit tape models. If students mistakenly count the number of measuring points instead of the number of parts, suggest they extend the lines to make them longer, then count the number of parts in which the can is divided. Students should label the lowest measuring point with a fraction, its denominator equaling the number of parts into which the can is divided, and its numerator being one. They should label the remaining measuring points with the same denominator and with numerators of two, three, and so on.

**2.** Students need not memorize the definitions or restate them formally. Allow for general descriptions in students' own words.

**Extension** You may discuss the different ways of naming one whole with a fraction by asking students to find the fractions that correspond to the full cans in problem **1.** [$\frac{5}{5}$, $\frac{2}{2}$, $\frac{4}{4}$, and $\frac{6}{6}$]

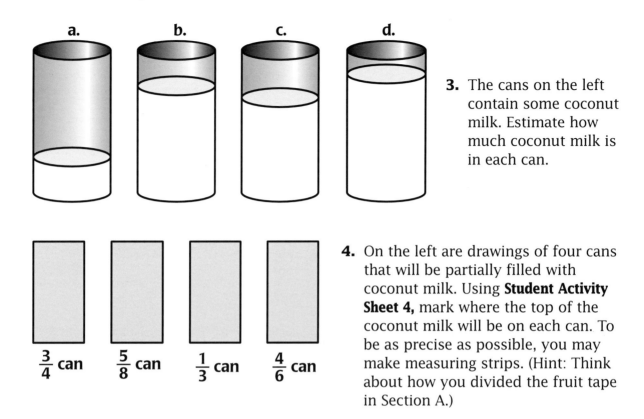

a.     b.     c.     d.

$\frac{3}{4}$ can    $\frac{5}{8}$ can    $\frac{1}{3}$ can    $\frac{4}{6}$ can

**3.** The cans on the left contain some coconut milk. Estimate how much coconut milk is in each can.

**4.** On the left are drawings of four cans that will be partially filled with coconut milk. Using **Student Activity Sheet 4,** mark where the top of the coconut milk will be on each can. To be as precise as possible, you may make measuring strips. (Hint: Think about how you divided the fruit tape in Section A.)

**5.** Collect some tin cans that are all the same size. Mark measuring lines on each can to show halves, thirds, fourths, sixths, eighths, and twelfths.

**6.** Suppose you have two cans of the same size that are partially filled with coconut milk. One can is $\frac{1}{2}$ full, and the other one is $\frac{1}{3}$ full. You want to pour the milk from the two cans into one empty can of the same size. Will one can hold all of this milk? How do you know?

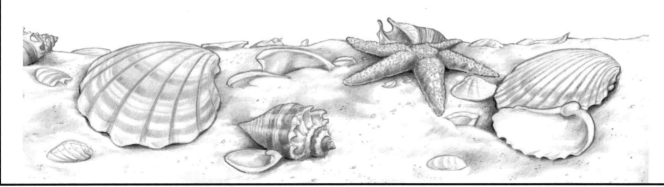

3. **a.** $\frac{1}{4}$

   **b.** $\frac{3}{4}$

   **c.** $\frac{2}{3}$

   **d.** $\frac{5}{6}$

4.

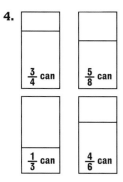

5. Check students' tin cans to be sure that each can is the same size and is properly labeled to show halves, thirds, fourths, sixths, eighths, and twelfths.

6. The milk will all fit into one can. Students may solve the problem in a variety of ways. Some possibilities follow:

   • Some students may solve the problem by actually pouring the two amounts of liquid into a can to see if one can will hold all of the liquid.

   • Some students may use measuring strips to model the problem.

   • Some students may use a drawing like the one pictured on the next student page.

   • Some students may reason as follows:

   If a can is half full, it has room for another half can of milk. Since one-third is less than one-half, the third will fit with a half into one can.

   If you pour the milk from the two cans into another can divided into sixths, it would be $\frac{5}{6}$ full.

**Materials** Student Activity Sheet 4 (one per student); tin cans or plastic/glass cylinders of the same size (six per pair of students); paper strips or string, optional (four per pair of students); scissors (one pair per student); tape, optional (one roll per pair of students); wooden sticks, optional (one per pair of students); waterproof markers, optional (one per pair of students)

**Overview** Students use fractions to estimate the amount of coconut milk in each of four cans. They begin to add fractions within the context of combining the contents of different cans.

**About the Mathematics** The model used for all of these problems is the fraction strip. The problems involve the following concepts:

• using fractions to estimate a quantity relative to a given whole,

• drawing the correct level on a can when a fraction is given,

• using fractions to describe different parts of a whole, and

• adding fractions informally.

**Planning** Students may work individually or in pairs on these problems. After they finish, briefly discuss the different estimation strategies that students used to solve the problems.

**Comments about the Problems**

3. Students may use estimation strategies such as the following:

   • They may cut paper measuring strips (or pieces of string) to match the size of the cans, mark the height of the liquid on the strip (string), and try to find the fraction by folding. This is similar to the fruit tape problems in Section A.

   • They may cut a small paper strip or piece of string; its length should correspond to either the height of the liquid or the empty part of the can. Find out how many times this strip or string fits into the height of the whole can. Note that this is not a general strategy; it will not work when a can is $\frac{3}{8}$ or $\frac{2}{5}$ full.

4. **Homework** This problem may be assigned as homework. Students can use measuring strips to solve this problem. Some students may make different strips for each problem; others may choose to use one strip for both **a** and **b** and another for parts **c** and **d** by folding an extra time.

5. Suggest that students make paper strips with lengths equal to the size of the cans. Have them fold the strips and label the folds with the appropriate fractions. The strips can be used as scales and taped outside the cans. Students can then use sticks to measure the amount of liquid in a can by holding a wet stick next to the measuring strip on the outside of the can and reading the fraction that corresponds to the water level.

Pete and Marge are on the island with you. Marge's can is filled $\frac{3}{4}$ of the way with coconut milk. Pete's can is filled $\frac{1}{3}$ of the way with coconut milk. They want to figure out if it is possible to put the contents of both cans together into one can of the same size.

Pete solves the problem in the following manner:

IF A CAN IS $\frac{3}{4}$ FULL, THERE IS STILL ROOM FOR $\frac{1}{4}$ OF A CAN. SINCE $\frac{1}{3}$ OF A CAN IS MORE THAN $\frac{1}{4}$ OF A CAN, I THINK THE COCONUT MILK WILL OVERFLOW.

Marge thinks about the problem in this way:

IF YOU DRAW THE TWO CANS AND SHADE THE AMOUNT OF MILK IN EACH, YOU CAN SEE THAT THE MILK IN CAN 2 WILL NOT ALL FIT INTO CAN 1.

7. Explain another way to solve the problem.

## Solutions and Samples
*of student work*

**7.** Answers will vary. Sample student responses:

- Fill one so that it is three-fourths full. Fill another can so that it is one-third full. Empty the liquid of both cans into an empty can and see if the liquid overflows.

- Make three paper strips of the same length. Divide one strip into fourths and shade three-fourths. Divide the second strip into thirds and shade one third. Line $\frac{3}{4}$ and $\frac{1}{3}$ up with the last strip to see if the two shaded areas are longer than one whole strip.

- Use a can or a measuring strip divided in twelfths and add the fractions $\frac{9}{12}$ and $\frac{4}{12}$ to see if together they are more than one whole.

## Hints and Comments

**Materials** Tin cans or glass/plastic cylinders from problem **5,** optional (six per pair of students); fraction strips from students' completed Student Activity Sheet 3, optional (one set per student)

**Overview** Students compare different strategies for solving problems that involve adding fractions with unlike denominators.

**About the Mathematics** Although you, as a teacher, use a formal algorithm for adding fractions with unlike denominators, some students may perform the addition on a more concrete level, using the tin cans. Others may add fractions using fraction strips. Allow students to use different strategies. Throughout this section, the emphasis shifts from using tin cans to using fraction strips. Students do not need to understand and use the formal algorithm for adding fractions with unlike denominators at this time.

**Planning** In problem **7,** students are not asked to find the total amount of milk in the two cans. They need only determine whether this amount is more than, less than, or equal to one whole can. Students may work on this problem individually or in pairs. When they finish, discuss students' solutions and strategies.

**Comments about the Problems**

**7.** If necessary, students may refer to their answers to problem **6.** Answers found using a concrete strategy (with real tin cans) are just as valid as those obtained using a more formal approach. Stress that it is not necessary to find the total amount of milk when the contents of both cans are combined.

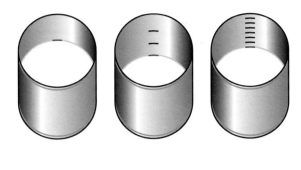

Suppose you have three cans of the same size partially filled with coconut milk. One can is $\frac{1}{2}$ full, the second is $\frac{1}{4}$ full, and the third is $\frac{1}{8}$ full.

**8.** Will the milk in these three cans fit into one can of the same size? Explain how you found your answer.

**9.** You have a can that is $\frac{1}{2}$ full, a can that is $\frac{1}{3}$ full, and a can that is $\frac{1}{4}$ full. Without pouring, how can you find out if the milk in these three cans will fit into one can of the same size?

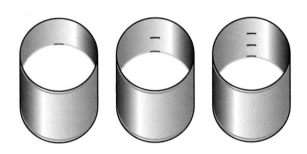

| can **a** | can **b** | can **c** |
|---|---|---|
| $\frac{2}{3}$ | $\frac{1}{2}$ | $\frac{1}{3}$ |
| full | full | full |

| can **d** | can **e** | can **f** |
|---|---|---|
| $\frac{1}{4}$ | $\frac{1}{6}$ | $\frac{1}{8}$ |
| full | full | full |

**10.** Suppose you have the six equal-sized cans of coconut milk shown on the left. The milk will not all fit into one can, but you can combine the milk of some of the cans. Write at least five combinations of cans whose milk could be poured together into one can of the same size. The milk does not have to fill a can completely.

**11.** Suppose you have two cans of the same size. One is $\frac{3}{4}$ full, and the other is $\frac{1}{4}$ full. If you combine the contents of the two cans, you will exactly fill one can of the same size. Find five ways to exactly fill one can using the cans in problem **10.** You may use cans more than once for each solution. Check your answers by using real cans.

RACTION TIMES

**Shipwrecked Kids Rescued**

8. All of the coconut milk will fit into one can of the same size. Explanations may be similar to those given for problems **6** and **7.**

9. The coconut milk will not all fit into one can. Explanations may be similar to those given for problems **6** and **7.**

10. Answers will vary. Sample answers:

| | |
|---|---|
| $a + c$ | $(\frac{2}{3} + \frac{1}{3})$ |
| $a + d$ | $(\frac{2}{3} + \frac{1}{4})$ |
| $a + e$ | $(\frac{2}{3} + \frac{1}{6})$ |
| $a + f$ | $(\frac{2}{3} + \frac{1}{8})$ |
| $b + c$ | $(\frac{1}{2} + \frac{1}{3})$ |
| $b + d$ | $(\frac{1}{2} + \frac{1}{4})$ |
| $b + e$ | $(\frac{1}{2} + \frac{1}{6})$ |
| $b + f$ | $(\frac{1}{2} + \frac{1}{8})$ |
| $c + d$ | $(\frac{1}{3} + \frac{1}{4})$ |
| $c + e$ | $(\frac{1}{3} + \frac{1}{6})$ |
| $c + f$ | $(\frac{1}{3} + \frac{1}{8})$ |
| $d + e$ | $(\frac{1}{4} + \frac{1}{6})$ |
| $d + f$ | $(\frac{1}{4} + \frac{1}{8})$ |
| $e + f$ | $(\frac{1}{6} + \frac{1}{8})$ |
| $b + c + f$ | $(\frac{1}{2} + \frac{1}{3} + \frac{1}{8})$ |
| $b + d + e$ | $(\frac{1}{2} + \frac{1}{4} + \frac{1}{6})$ |
| $b + d + f$ | $(\frac{1}{2} + \frac{1}{4} + \frac{1}{8})$ |
| $c + d + e$ | $(\frac{1}{3} + \frac{1}{4} + \frac{1}{6})$ |
| $c + d + f$ | $(\frac{1}{3} + \frac{1}{4} + \frac{1}{8})$ |
| $c + e + f$ | $(\frac{1}{3} + \frac{1}{6} + \frac{1}{8})$ |
| $d + e + f$ | $(\frac{1}{4} + \frac{1}{6} + \frac{1}{8})$ |
| $c + d + e + f$ | $(\frac{1}{3} + \frac{1}{4} + \frac{1}{6} + \frac{1}{8})$ |

11. Answers will vary. Sample answers:

| | |
|---|---|
| $a + c$ | $(\frac{2}{3} + \frac{1}{3})$ |
| $b + d + d$ | $(\frac{1}{2} + \frac{1}{4} + \frac{1}{4})$ |
| $b + d + f + f$ | $(\frac{1}{2} + \frac{1}{4} + \frac{1}{8} + \frac{1}{8})$ |
| $b + e + e + e$ | $(\frac{1}{2} + \frac{1}{6} + \frac{1}{6} + \frac{1}{6})$ |
| $c + c + e + e$ | $(\frac{1}{3} + \frac{1}{3} + \frac{1}{6} + \frac{1}{6})$ |
| $b + c + e$ | $(\frac{1}{2} + \frac{1}{3} + \frac{1}{6})$ |

**Materials** Tin cans or glass/plastic cylinders from problem **5,** optional (six per pair or group of students); fraction strips from students' completed Student Activity Sheet 3, optional (one set per student)

**Overview** Students investigate combining the contents of different cans to determine which cans' contents, when poured together, add up to one can or less.

**About the Mathematics** These problems extend problems **6** and **7** in two ways:

• Students combine the contents of more than two cans. They informally add more than two fractions.

• Students look for combinations that will fit into or exactly fill one whole can. They work with fractions that together make less than one or exactly one whole.

**Planning** Students may use the cans from problem **5.** They may work in pairs or in small groups on these problems. Problems **9** and **10** may be used for assessment and/or assigned as homework.

**Comments about the Problems**

8–10. **Informal Assessment** These problems assess students' ability to use informal strategies for operations with fractions. Students may need to use real cans to find or check their answers. They may also draw cans or use fraction strips. If students are having difficulty, have them refer to the strategies described on page 10 of the Student Book.

10. Some students may need to use tin cans or fraction strips, while others are able to reason on a more formal level using fraction notation. Students will give answers on different levels. Some may list only a few easy, two-can combinations; others may generate a lengthy list. Once again, it is important for students to share their solutions and strategies.

11. If this problem is challenging for some students, encourage them to find only two or three possibilities and then share them with the rest of the group or class. You may also want students to check their answers using the tin cans. Again, answers may be given on different levels.

**Extension** Ask students to develop a systematic strategy for finding all possible combinations of two, three, four, five, and six cans in problem **10.**

# FRACTIONS and MORE FRACTIONS

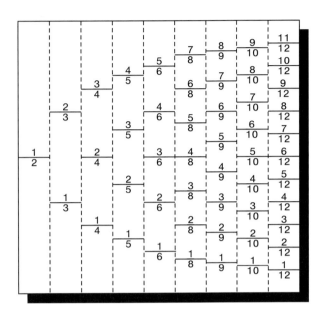

Suppose you have nine tin cans of the same size. Each can has the same height as the measuring strips on **Student Activity Sheet 5.** You can use these strips to draw measuring lines inside the cans.

Cut out the strips on **Student Activity Sheet 5.** Use the strips to find out what will happen if you pour coconut milk from two or more cans into one can.

**12. a.** Suppose you poured $\frac{1}{3}$ of a can of milk and $\frac{1}{2}$ of a can of milk into another can of the same size. How can you use your fraction strips to find how full the other can will be?

   **b.** Explain why this sentence is correct: $\frac{1}{3}$ can $+ \frac{1}{2}$ can $= \frac{5}{6}$ can.

**13. a.** Use the strips to find at least six fraction combinations like the one in problem **12b.** Write a sentence for each.

   **b.** For each sentence, explain why it is correct.

You may have included a sentence in problem **13** with an outcome of more than one, such as this sentence: $\frac{3}{4}$ can $+ \frac{1}{2}$ can $= 1\frac{1}{4}$ can.

Numbers like $1\frac{1}{4}$ are called **mixed numbers**.

**14.** Why do you think numbers like $1\frac{1}{4}$ and $2\frac{3}{5}$ are called *mixed numbers*?

**12. a.** The other can will be five-sixths full. Some students may see that when they place their strip that is divided into thirds next to their strip that is divided into sixths, $\frac{1}{3}$ matches with $\frac{2}{6}$. Likewise, when they place their strip that is divided into halves next to the one that is divided into sixths, $\frac{1}{2}$ matches with $\frac{3}{6}$. Students can line up the measuring strips to see whether two fractions make more or less than one whole strip.

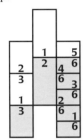

Students will see that $\frac{1}{3}$ can and $\frac{1}{2}$ can are more than $\frac{2}{3}$ can and less than one whole can. Now they can match the height with the other strip and find that the amounts add up to $\frac{5}{6}$ can.

**b.** Explanations will vary. Possible explanations:

Since $\frac{1}{3}$ can = $\frac{2}{6}$ can, and $\frac{1}{2}$ can = $\frac{3}{6}$ can, then $\frac{1}{3}$ can + $\frac{1}{2}$ can = $\frac{2}{6}$ can + $\frac{3}{6}$ can, or $\frac{5}{6}$ can.

When I poured $\frac{1}{3}$ can and $\frac{1}{2}$ can into a can divided into six equal parts, the liquid filled the can up to the $\frac{5}{6}$ mark.

**13. a.** Answers will vary. Sample answers:

$\frac{1}{3}$ can + $\frac{1}{6}$ can = $\frac{3}{6}$ can

$\frac{3}{4}$ can + $\frac{3}{8}$ can = $1\frac{1}{8}$ cans

$\frac{1}{2}$ can + $\frac{1}{4}$ can = $\frac{3}{4}$ can

**b.** Explanations will vary. Possible explanations:

Since $\frac{1}{3}$ can = $\frac{2}{6}$ can, $\frac{1}{3}$ can + $\frac{1}{6}$ can = $\frac{2}{6}$ can + $\frac{1}{6}$ can, or $\frac{3}{6}$ can.

Since $\frac{3}{4}$ can = $\frac{6}{8}$ can, $\frac{3}{4}$ can + $\frac{3}{8}$ can = $\frac{6}{8}$ can + $\frac{3}{8}$ can, or $1\frac{1}{8}$ can.

Since $\frac{1}{2}$ can = $\frac{2}{4}$ can, $\frac{1}{2}$ can + $\frac{1}{4}$ can = $\frac{2}{4}$ can + $\frac{1}{4}$ can, or $\frac{3}{4}$ can.

**14.** Answers may vary. Possible student response:

They are called mixed numbers because they have a whole number and a fraction.

**Materials** Student Activity Sheet 5 (one per student); scissors (one pair per student); transparency of Student Activity Sheet 5, optional (one per class); magic markers, optional (one set per class); fraction strips from students' completed Student Activity Sheet 3, optional (one set per student)

**Overview** Students use fractions to express the total amount of milk when the contents of two cans are poured together.

**About the Mathematics** Students make the transition from working on the concrete level using tin cans, to working more formally with fraction strips. Adding fractions is still related to the context of combining the contents of cans, but a more formal fraction notation is introduced. Fractions are always labeled: $\frac{1}{2}$ can + $\frac{1}{3}$ can = $\frac{5}{6}$ can, instead of $\frac{1}{2} + \frac{1}{3} = \frac{5}{6}$. Students should also recognize that a whole can may be named in different ways: $\frac{2}{2}, \frac{3}{3}, \frac{4}{4}$, and so on.

**Planning** You may want to prepare a transparency of Student Activity Sheet 5 and color the fraction strips with different colors. Students can then share their solutions to problem **13** on the overhead. Tell them to cut out whole fraction strips. Students may work on these problems individually or in pairs. Be sure to discuss the solutions and strategies for problem **12** before students begin problem **13**. Problem **14** should be discussed along with problem **15** on the next page.

**Comments about the Problems**

**12.** Students may use fraction strips to find relationships between the fractions. Do not require that they use formal algorithms. Let them check their solutions by reasoning in terms of cans or fraction strips.

**13. Informal Assessment** This problem assesses students' ability to use informal strategies for operations with fractions and to use fractions to describe part-whole relationships. It also assesses their understanding of and ability to use the relationships between benchmark fractions.

If students are having difficulty with this problem, it may be helpful to have them relate the strips to the markings on the tin cans.

**14.** You may want to compare $1\frac{1}{4}$ and $2\frac{3}{5}$ to one whole (or to two wholes). Make sure that students are able to correctly interpret the meaning of mixed numbers: $1\frac{1}{4}$ means 1 whole + $\frac{1}{4}$ of a whole, and $2\frac{3}{5}$ means 2 wholes + $\frac{3}{5}$ of a whole.

Devin, a student in Ms. Wood's class, wrote the following sentence:

$$\tfrac{3}{4} \text{ can} + \tfrac{1}{2} \text{ can} = \tfrac{5}{4} \text{ can}$$

**15.** Is Devin's sentence correct? Explain.

Devin and Becky both lost their paper strips from **Student Activity Sheet 5.** They made the new strips you see below.

**16. a.** Are both sets of strips okay to use to measure amounts of coconut milk? Explain why or why not.

**b.** Devin found a quarter strip from **Student Activity Sheet 5.** How can Devin decide whether or not he can use this strip with the new strips he just made to solve fraction problems?

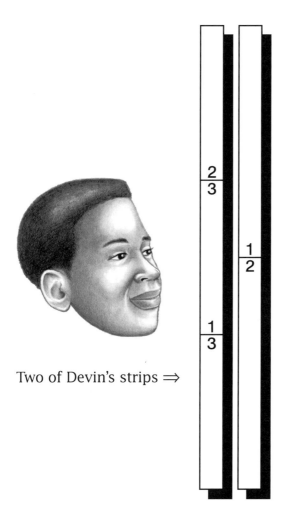

Two of Devin's strips ⟹

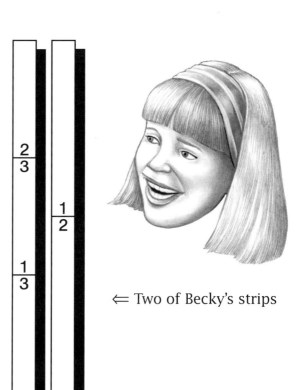

⟸ Two of Becky's strips

**15.** Yes. The fraction $\frac{5}{4}$ is the same as $1\frac{1}{4}$. Explanations will vary. Possible explanations:

- The fraction $\frac{1}{2}$ is the same as $\frac{2}{4}$ (using cans or fraction strips), so $\frac{3}{4}$ can and $\frac{2}{4}$ can together are the same as $\frac{5}{4}$ can.

- You can line up the fraction strips that show $\frac{3}{4}$ and $\frac{1}{2}$ and then use the fraction strip showing fourths to see how many fourths they equal. The result is shown below:

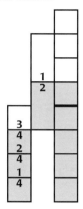

**16. a.** Yes, both sets of strips are okay to use for measuring. The important fact is that you cannot mix the strips from the two different sets.

**b.** Devin could compare $\frac{2}{4}$ of the strip from Student Activity Sheet 5 with $\frac{1}{2}$ on the strip he made. If two of the fourths on the quarter strip are equal to one-half of his new strip, then he can use the quarter strip.

**Materials** fraction strips from students' completed Student Activity Sheet 3, optional (one set per student)

**Overview** Students explore two different ways to write fractions greater than one. They also compare fraction strips of different lengths.

**About the Mathematics** Problems **14** and **15** provide students with a mathematical way to talk about fractional quantities greater than one, using *mixed numbers.* A mixed number is made up of a whole number and a fraction, such as $1\frac{1}{4}$, which can also be written as $\frac{5}{4}$. Fractions such as $\frac{5}{4}$, in which the numerator is always larger than the denominator, are called *improper fractions.* It is not important for students to use these terms, since this unit serves as only an introduction to fractions. Problem **16** addresses the concept that fractions are relative to the size of the whole. One-half of a large fraction strip is bigger than one-half of a smaller fraction strip.

**Planning** Students can work on these problems individually or in pairs. Discuss students' solutions and explanations for problems **15** and **16.**

**Comments about the Problems**

**15.** Students may reason on different levels: on a concrete level using cans, on a semi-concrete level using strips, or on a more formal level using fractions. For examples, see the Solutions column on this page.

**16. Informal Assessment** This problem assesses students' understanding of the relative nature of fractions. It may be helpful to refer to the context of real cans to clarify the relative nature of fractions. Half of one large can contains as much as $\frac{2}{4}$ of one large can. The same is true for a small can. However, half of a small can contains less than half of a large can, so large and small cans cannot be mixed.

# Summary

When a whole is divided equally into parts, you can use fractions to describe the parts. The top number in a fraction is called the *numerator.* The bottom number is called the *denominator.*

It is possible to combine fractions. One possibility is:

$$\tfrac{1}{2} \text{ can} + \tfrac{1}{4} \text{ can} = \tfrac{3}{4} \text{ can}$$

Measuring strips can help you combine fractions. If you write fractions beside measuring points on cans, you usually do it like this:

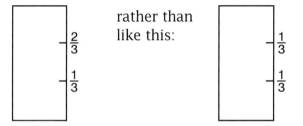

rather than like this:

## Summary Questions

You and your friends are sharing subs. You get $\frac{4}{3}$ of a sub. One of your friends gets $\frac{2}{3}$ of a sub.

**17. a.** What does $\frac{4}{3}$ mean?

   **b.** How is $\frac{2}{3}$ related to $\frac{4}{3}$?

**18.** Look at the numerators in the sentence $\frac{1}{2}$ can $+ \frac{1}{4}$ can $= \frac{3}{4}$ can. How is it possible to get a 3 as the numerator?

**19.** You and a friend go out for pizza. You order a 10-inch pepperoni pizza and an 8-inch cheese pizza. Both pizzas are cut into eight equal slices. You eat six pepperoni and two cheese slices. Your friend eats the rest. Who ate more pizza, you or your friend? Explain.

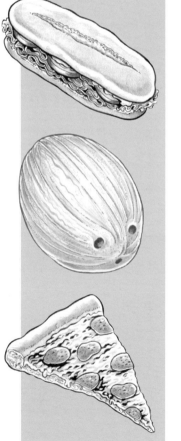

**17. a.** Answers will vary. Sample student responses:

$\frac{4}{3} = 1$ sub $+ \frac{1}{3}$ sub

Each sub is divided into three pieces. I get four pieces.

**b.** Answers will vary. Sample responses:

$\frac{2}{3}$ is half of $\frac{4}{3}$.

$\frac{4}{3}$ is two times larger than $\frac{2}{3}$.

**18.** Answers will vary. Possible answer:

To combine $\frac{1}{2}$ can and $\frac{1}{4}$ can into a single fraction of a can, both cans need to be divided into the same number of equal parts. If I divide each of the two equal parts in half, I get a total of four equal parts. Instead of $\frac{1}{2}$ can $+ \frac{1}{4}$ can, I can write $\frac{2}{4}$ can $+ \frac{1}{4}$ can to get $\frac{3}{4}$ can.

**19.** You ate more pizza. Explanations will vary. You and your friend both ate the same number of slices, but the pepperoni slices were bigger than the cheese slices.

**Materials** fraction strips from students' completed Student Activity Sheet 3, optional (one set per student)

**Overview** Students read the Summary, which reviews the main concepts of this section. They solve fraction problems within the context of sharing food.

**About the Mathematics** In addition to the main concepts outlined in the Summary, students were also informally introduced to the concepts of *mixed numbers* and *improper fractions* in this section. As earlier stated, it is not important that students know and use these terms, since this is an introductory unit on fractions.

**Planning** Students may work on problems **17–19** individually or in pairs. These problems may be assigned as homework. You may use problems **18** and **19** as assessment. After students complete Section B, you may assign appropriate activities in the Try This! section, located on pages 38–41 of the Student Book, for homework.

**Comments about the Problems**

**17. Homework** This problem may be assigned as homework. Allow students to solve this problem on different levels. Some students may need to use cans and/or fraction strips.

**18. Informal Assessment** This problem assesses students' understanding of and ability to use the relationships between benchmark fractions. Students' explanations will vary. Some students may base their answers on their work with cans. Others will use fraction strips or reason with fractions: "$\frac{1}{2}$ can $+ \frac{1}{4}$ can $= \frac{2}{4}$ can $+ \frac{1}{4}$ can $= \frac{3}{4}$ can, so the three indicates three parts out of four."

**19. Informal Assessment** This problem assesses students' understanding of the relative nature of fractions, as well as their ability to estimate fractions and parts of wholes and to solve contextual problems in which simple fractions are involved, using informal strategies. Students should realize that they cannot combine fractional amounts in this situation, since the pizzas are of different sizes. For example, a one-eighth slice from the large pizza cannot be added to a one-eighth slice from the small pizza.

**Extension** Ask students to create an appropriate test problem similar to those in this section. Then ask students to solve their problems themselves. You may want to use some student problems for assessment later in the unit.

## Work Students Do

Within the context of modifying the amounts of recipe ingredient to allow for different serving sizes, students informally add, subtract, multiply, and divide fractions. They read a pizza recipe that makes four pizzas and determine how to modify the amounts of each ingredient to make 24 pizzas. The *ratio table* is introduced as a model to show how the amount of each ingredient changes as the number of servings changes. Students then use a ratio table to determine the ingredient amounts for different servings of another recipe. At the end of this section, students work with metric measurements for volume, using liters and deciliters.

## Goals

**Students will:**

- recognize part-whole relationships;
- use informal strategies for operations with fractions;
- use equivalent forms of benchmark fractions within a context;
- develop an understanding of and use the relationships between benchmark fractions;
- solve contextual problems in which simple fractions are involved, using informal strategies.

## Pacing

- approximately three 45-minute class sessions

## Vocabulary

- deciliter
- liter
- ratio table
- volume

## About the Mathematics

Operations with fractions are the main focus of this section. Students apply informal strategies to increase or reduce the serving sizes of recipes using the *ratio table* model. The ratio table serves two primary purposes. First, the table builds upon students' informal strategies for performing operations with fractions, like halving and doubling. Second, the ratio table is a useful tool for organizing fraction calculations. Though the concept of ratio is implied throughout the section, it is not the intent of this unit for students to gain a complete understanding of ratios. In the grade 5/6 unit *Grasping Sizes,* the concept of ratio is made more explicit.

By modifying the amounts of ingredients in a recipe as the serving size changes, students may begin to understand constant relationships. For example, if a recipe calls for one cup of sugar and two cups of flour and the recipe is then doubled or halved, the relationship of cups of sugar to cups of flour remains constant, as shown in the ratio table below:

| Cups of Flour | 1 | 2 | 3 | 4 |
|---|---|---|---|---|
| Cups of Sugar | $\frac{1}{2}$ | 1 | $1\frac{1}{2}$ | 2 |

This relationship can also be described as follows: cups of flour $= 2 \times$ cups of sugar.

The metric units *liter* and *deciliter* are introduced at the end of the section. A measuring cup marked in liters and deciliters is used to relate the metric divisions of tenths to the standard divisions of $\frac{1}{3}$ and $\frac{2}{3}$ cup. The metric system and decimal concepts are further developed in the grade 5/6 unit *Measure for Measure.*

## Materials

- Student Activity Sheets 6–8, pages 108–110 of the Teacher Guide (one of each per student)
- set of standard measuring cups, page 39 of the Teacher Guide, optional (one set per class)
- fraction strips, pages 39, 47, 49, and 51 of the Teacher Guide, optional (one set per student)
- one-liter measuring cup, page 49 of the Teacher Guide, optional (one per class)
- additional recipes, pages 41, 47, and 53 of the Teacher Guide, optional (one per student)

## Planning Instruction

You might want to begin by having a short discussion about the context of this section, modifying the amounts of recipe ingredients to make different-sized servings. Ask students: *Have you ever had to help cook for a group of people that was larger or smaller than the recipe's serving size? What did you do?* See other discussion suggestions in the Planning section on page 41 of the Teacher Guide. Some solutions in the Teacher Guide are written with formal fraction and operation symbols, but students are not required to use fraction notation to express their answers. Some students may write their answers in a sentence such as *half of one-half is one-fourth.* Students are not expected to master operations with fractions by the end of this section.

Students may work individually or in pairs on problems 2, 8–13, and 14–16. They may work in pairs or in small groups on the remaining problems.

There are no optional problems in this section.

## Homework

Problems 9 (page 46 of the Teacher Guide), 14–16 (page 50 of the Teacher Guide), and 18 (page 52 of the Teacher Guide) can be assigned as homework. The Extensions (pages 39, 45, 47, 49, and 51 of the Teacher Guide) and the Bringing Math Home activity (page 41 of the Teacher Guide) can also be assigned as homework. After students complete Section C, you may assign appropriate activities from the Try This! section located on pages 38–41 of the *Some of the Parts* Student Book. The Try This! activities reinforce the key math concepts introduced in this section.

## Planning Assessment

- Problem 8 can be used to informally assess students' ability to use informal strategies for operations with fractions and their understanding of and ability to use the relationships between benchmark fractions.
- Problem 13 can be used to informally assess students' ability to use equivalent forms of benchmark fractions within a context.
- Problem 14b can be used to informally assess students' ability to recognize part-whole relationships.
- Problem 18 can be used to informally assess students' ability to solve contextual problems in which simple fractions are involved, using informal strategies and their ability to use informal strategies for operations with fractions.

## C. FRACTIONS AND RECIPES

# Standard Measures

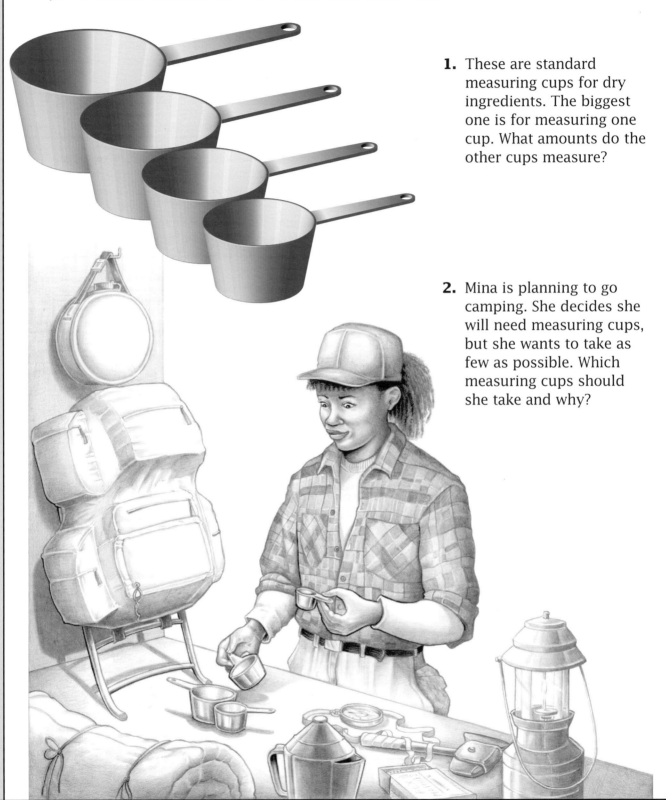

1. These are standard measuring cups for dry ingredients. The biggest one is for measuring one cup. What amounts do the other cups measure?

2. Mina is planning to go camping. She decides she will need measuring cups, but she wants to take as few as possible. Which measuring cups should she take and why?

1. The answer cannot be determined from the drawings since not only the heights, but the diameters of the cups must be considered. A good guess might be $\frac{1}{2}$ cup, $\frac{1}{3}$ cup, and $\frac{1}{4}$ cup.

2. Answers will vary. Sample student responses:

   With a $\frac{1}{4}$ measuring cup, she can also make $\frac{1}{2}$ and 1 cup. So she needs to take only the $\frac{1}{4}$ and $\frac{1}{3}$ measuring cups.

   She needs to take only the 1 cup measuring cup. To measure amounts that are less than 1 cup, she can estimate.

**Materials** set of standard measuring cups, optional (one set per classroom); fraction strips, optional (one set per student)

**Overview** Students think about standard measuring cups and the fractional amount that each size cup might hold. Measuring cups are used in the recipes throughout this section.

**About the Mathematics** In the United States and Great Britain, recipe ingredients are often measured using standard measuring cups. Fractional amounts, like $\frac{1}{4}$ cup, play an important role in recipes in these countries. In countries that use the metric system, recipe ingredients are measured in deciliters (one-tenth of a liter) and milliliters (one-thousandth of a liter), and decimal numbers like 0.3 liters are common. Later in this section, the liter and deciliter are introduced, and the concept of "tenths" receives more attention. Using metric units prepares students for the use of decimals in the unit *Measure for Measure*.

**Planning** Problem **1** is best done in class. Students may work on problem **2** individually or in pairs.

**Comments about the Problems**

1. Some students may be familiar with standard measuring cups. Make sure that all students know the correct fractional name for each size cup. To help students compare the relative size of the measuring cups, ask questions such as: *How many one-third cups are needed to fill one cup?* [three] *How many one-fourth cups?* [four] It may help students to compare $\frac{1}{3}$ and $\frac{1}{4}$ using their fraction strips. However, some students may have difficulty making the connection between the measuring cups and the fraction strips.

2. There are no right or wrong answers to this problem.

**Extension** Ask students to compile a list of the different amounts that can be measured using this set of measuring cups. For example, $\frac{2}{3}$ of a cup can be measured by using the $\frac{1}{3}$ cup twice. Also, $\frac{5}{6}$ of a cup can be measured by combining $\frac{1}{3}$ cup and $\frac{1}{2}$ cup. This problem is similar to the problems in Section B that involve combining the contents of cans.

Juan found the following pizza recipe.

# Pizza Patterns

*Makes 4 pizzas.*

### Ingredients
1 8-fl oz jar of spaghetti sauce
1 lb ground beef
$\frac{1}{3}$ cup dry bread crumbs
$\frac{1}{2}$ tsp dried oregano
2 pitted ripe olives
$\frac{1}{4}$ cup shredded mozzarella cheese
$\frac{1}{4}$ cup shredded cheddar cheese
4 mushrooms

### Utensils
Liquid measuring cup
Medium bowl
Dry measuring cup
Measuring spoons
Fork
Shallow baking pan, $15\frac{1}{2}'' \times 10\frac{1}{2}''$
Ruler
Spatula
Sharp knife
Cutting board
Pot holders

1. Preheat oven to 425°F.
2. Measure $\frac{1}{2}$ cup (4 fl oz) from the jar of spaghetti sauce. Save the rest of the jar of sauce.
3. Add the $\frac{1}{2}$ cup spaghetti sauce, 1 lb ground beef, $\frac{1}{3}$ cup dry bread crumbs, and $\frac{1}{2}$ teaspoon dried oregano to bowl and stir with a fork until mixed together. Divide the mixture into four equal balls. Place each ball several inches apart in the baking pan.
4. Pat each ball into a $4\frac{1}{2}$-inch circle. Pinch the edge of each circle to make a rim.
5. Pour about 2 tablespoons of the remaining spaghetti sauce into the center of each circle and spread it to the edges with a spatula. Bake 15 to 20 minutes.
6. While the pizzas are baking, cut 2 pitted ripe olives and 4 mushrooms crosswise into 4 slices each.
7. Remove the pan from the oven.
8. Sprinkle each pizza with $\frac{1}{4}$ cup shredded mozzarella cheese and $\frac{1}{4}$ cup shredded cheddar cheese, dividing the cheese over the four pizzas. Make a pattern on each pizza using 4 mushroom slices and 2 olive slices per pizza.
9. Remove pizzas from the oven, turn the oven off, and let pizzas cool before eating.

HINT: BE CREATIVE AND USE YOUR FAVORITE FOODS TO MAKE ALL TYPES OF PATTERNS.

**Materials** additional recipes, optional (one per student)

**Overview** Students read a pizza recipe, which provides a context for introducing the ratio table model.

**About the Mathematics** The *ratio table* model is introduced on page 42 of this Teacher Guide. With a ratio table, equivalent ratios can be found by means of halving, doubling, multiplying, dividing, adding, or subtracting. Students will use a ratio table to determine the amounts of each ingredient in a pizza recipe when serving sizes change. Here is an example of a ratio table that shows the number of mushrooms needed for different recipe servings of pizza:

| Number of Pizzas | 1 | 2 | 3 | 4 |
|---|---|---|---|---|
| Number of Mushrooms | 4 | 8 | 12 | 16 |

**Planning** You may want to have a short discussion about students' cooking experiences to introduce the context of recipes. Ask students: *Have you ever cooked, and if so, what did you cook? Did you use a recipe?*

You can continue by reading the recipe aloud. If necessary, explain the meaning of any unfamiliar ingredients or utensils as you read.

**Bringing Math Home** You may ask students to obtain parental permission to actually make the Pizza Patterns recipe at home. You might also ask students to bring copies of their favorite recipes from home to school. These recipes can then be used to create additional problems, similar to those in this section.

**Did You Know?** Pizza originated in Naples as a simple circle of dough topped with olive oil, tomatoes, and mozzarella cheese that was baked quickly in a hot oven. It was made popular in the United States by the Italian community in New York City, where the first U.S. pizzeria opened in 1905.

Juan makes a pizza and likes the taste of it so much that he decides to have a pizza party. He invites 23 friends. The recipe makes four pizzas, but Juan decides that he will need to make 24 pizza patterns. All of his friends love pizza.

**3.** What will Juan have to do to the amount of each ingredient to make 24 pizzas?

**4.** How much shredded cheddar cheese will he need to make 24 pizzas?

| Number of Pizzas | 4 | | |
|---|---|---|---|
| Teaspoons of Oregano | $\frac{1}{2}$ | | |

Ming, one of Juan's friends, helps him prepare the food. She starts with the oregano. She makes a table to show how the amount of oregano will change as the number of pizzas changes.

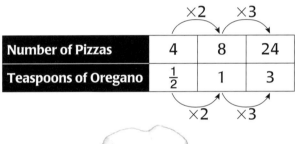

| Number of Pizzas | 4 | 8 | 24 |
|---|---|---|---|
| Teaspoons of Oregano | $\frac{1}{2}$ | 1 | 3 |

Ming multiplies the number of pizzas and teaspoons of oregano by two and then multiplies again by three. The table on the left shows how Ming found the number of teaspoons of oregano needed for 24 pizzas.

**3.** Strategies will vary. Sample strategies:

Multiply the amount of each ingredient by six. For example, multiply $\frac{1}{3}$ cup dry bread crumbs by six: $\frac{1}{3} \times 6 = \frac{6}{3} = 2$ cups.

Double the amount of each ingredient. Then multiply those amounts by three. For example, double $\frac{1}{3}$ cup dry bread crumbs: $\frac{1}{3} + \frac{1}{3} = \frac{2}{3}$.

Multiply that amount by three: $\frac{2}{3} \times 3 = \frac{6}{3} = 2$ cups.

Double the amount of each ingredient. Then double that amount. Add the two amounts. For example, take $\frac{1}{3}$ cup dry bread crumbs:

Double the amount: $\frac{1}{3} + \frac{1}{3} = \frac{2}{3}$

Double that amount: $\frac{2}{3} + \frac{2}{3} = \frac{4}{3}$

Add the two amounts: $\frac{2}{3} + \frac{4}{3} = \frac{6}{3} = 2$ cups.

**4.** $1\frac{1}{2}$ cups of shredded cheddar cheese

**Overview** Students determine the amounts needed for two ingredients in a pizza recipe whose serving size changes. The ratio table is introduced in an example. Students study and use ratio tables throughout this section.

**About the Mathematics** The concept of *ratio* is formally introduced in the unit *Grasping Sizes*. The ratio table model is used here as a tool to organize computations with fractions. One advantage of the ratio table is that it provides an open structure for students to use their own steps when working toward a solution. The different methods of calculating in a ratio table are addressed in this section. The term *ratio table* is discussed on the next page.

**Planning** Students should work on problems **3** and **4** before they study the ratio tables. Discuss students' strategies for solving problem **4;** this problem prepares students for the strategies used in the ratio table. The two ratio table examples can then be read and discussed in class. Students may work in pairs or in small groups on these problems.

**Comments about the Problems**

**3.** It is crucial for students to remember that the given recipe's ingredient amounts will make four pizzas.

**4.** Let students develop their own strategies for finding out how much six times $\frac{1}{4}$ is. They can use their strips to see that four-fourths make one whole, and that the remaining two-fourths make $\frac{1}{2}$. Other strategies are possible. Do not emphasize formal algorithms at this point. For the ratio tables on the next page, calculations are written more formally. Students can also apply their own strategies in these ratio tables.

Juan's friend Katrina looked at Ming's table and said,

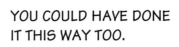

YOU COULD HAVE DONE IT THIS WAY TOO.

| | $\times 6$ | |
| --- | --- | --- |
| **Number of Pizzas** | 4 | 24 |
| **Teaspoons of Oregano** | $\frac{1}{2}$ | 3 |

$\times 6$

**5.** How did Katrina figure out that $\frac{1}{2} \times 6 = 3$?

Katrina figured out the amount of oregano needed for 24 pizzas in still another way.

| | $\times 2$ | $\times 2$ | $8 + 16$ | |
| --- | --- | --- | --- | --- |
| **Number of Pizzas** | 4 | 8 | 16 | 24 |
| **Teaspoons of Oregano** | $\frac{1}{2}$ | 1 | 2 | 3 |
| | $\times 2$ | $\times 2$ | $1 + 2$ | |

**6. a.** Explain Katrina's strategy.

**b.** How are Katrina's and Ming's strategies different? How are they alike?

| | | | |
| --- | --- | --- | --- |
| **Number of Pizzas** | 4 | | |
| **Cups of Bread Crumbs** | $\frac{1}{3}$ | | |
| **Jars of Spaghetti Sauce** | 1 | | |
| **Pounds of Ground Beef** | 1 | | |
| **Teaspoons of Dried Oregano** | $\frac{1}{2}$ | | |
| **Number of Olives** | 2 | | |
| **Cups of Shredded Mozzarella Cheese** | $\frac{1}{4}$ | | |
| **Cups of Shredded Cheddar Cheese** | $\frac{1}{4}$ | | |
| **Number of Mushrooms** | 4 | | |

The tables Katrina and Ming made are called **ratio tables**. The table on the left is like a ratio table, except with more ingredients listed.

**7.** Complete the table on **Student Activity Sheet 6** so that Juan and his friends can make 24 pizza patterns.

**5.** Answers will vary. Sample student responses:

Maybe she knew that $\frac{1}{2}$ teaspoon and $\frac{1}{2}$ teaspoon makes one teaspoon, and she needed six $\frac{1}{2}$s, so six times $\frac{1}{2}$ equals 3 teaspoons.

$\frac{1}{2}$ tsp + $\frac{1}{2}$ tsp = 1 tsp

$\frac{1}{2}$ tsp + $\frac{1}{2}$ tsp = 1 tsp

$\frac{1}{2}$ tsp + $\frac{1}{2}$ tsp = 1 tsp

If she knew that two times one-half is one teaspoon and three times two is six, then she could figure that three times one teaspoon equals three teaspoons.

**6. a.** Answers will vary. Sample student response:

Katrina doubled the number of pizzas twice and doubled the number of teaspoons of oregano twice. She then added the numbers in the second and third columns so that there would be enough oregano for 24 pizzas.

**b.** Answers will vary. Possible answer:

Their strategies are different because Ming multiplied to figure the amount of oregano and Katrina multiplied and added. They are alike because both strategies show the relationship between the numbers of pizzas and teaspoons of oregano in each column.

**7.** Answers will vary. Some students may use a doubling or adding strategy while others might multiply. Sample student response:

$\times 2$   $\times 2$

| Number of Pizzas | 4 | 8 | 16 | 24 |
|---|---|---|---|---|
| Cups of Bread Crumbs | $\frac{1}{3}$ | $\frac{2}{3}$ | $\frac{4}{3}$ | 2 |
| Jars of Spaghetti Sauce | 1 | 2 | 4 | 6 |
| Pounds of Ground Beef | 1 | 2 | 4 | 6 |
| Teaspoons of Dried Oregano | $\frac{1}{2}$ | 1 | 2 | 3 |
| Number of Olives | 2 | 4 | 8 | 12 |
| Cups of Shredded Mozzarella Cheese | $\frac{1}{4}$ | $\frac{1}{2}$ | 1 | $1\frac{1}{2}$ |
| Cups of Shredded Cheddar Cheese | $\frac{1}{4}$ | $\frac{1}{2}$ | 1 | $1\frac{1}{2}$ |
| Number of Mushrooms | 4 | 8 | 16 | 24 |

add

$\times 6$

**Materials** Student Activity Sheet 6 (one per student)

**Overview** Students study different strategies used in a ratio table to compute with fractions. They also choose their own strategies for completing a ratio table.

**About the Mathematics** Strategies used so far for completing a ratio table include:
- doubling columns,
- multiplying a column by a whole number,
- adding columns,
- halving columns,
- dividing a column by a (whole) number, and
- subtracting columns.

Students may come up with these additional strategies when solving problem **7**. Be sure that students realize that they cannot add to or subtract from an individual quantity in one column of a ratio table without affecting the ratio relationship between the top and the bottom numbers in that column.

**Planning** You may want to clarify the term *ratio table* for students by explaining that the relationship between the number of pizzas and the amounts of ingredients must remain constant, even if the numbers themselves change. For example, you will always need $\frac{1}{2}$ teaspoon of oregano for each "group" of four pizzas, even though you may make a total of 12 pizzas. Students do not need to know the formal definition of ratio or ratio table. More practice with ratio tables can be found in *Number Tools*. Discuss students' solutions for problems **6** and **7**.

**Comments about the Problems**

**5.** Students can use different strategies. If they are having difficulty, encourage them to use their fraction strips.

**6.** Allow students to write explanations in their own words.

**7.** If students have difficulty with a ratio table this large, suggest that they make a separate ratio table for each ingredient. Each table should be labeled to show the number of pizzas in the top row and the amount of each ingredient in the bottom row. If students find that they need more steps and, therefore, more columns, let them extend the ratio table to the right.

**Extension** You may ask students to return to problem **4** in this section and solve it using a ratio table.

# Yogurt Cups

*Makes 4 cups.*

**Ingredients**

$\frac{3}{4}$ cup all-purpose flour
$\frac{1}{4}$ cup margarine or butter, softened
3 Tbs powdered sugar
2 to 3 Tbs cold water
$1\frac{1}{3}$ cups yogurt (any flavor)

1. Heat oven to 375°F.

2. Mix flour, margarine, and powdered sugar until crumbly. Sprinkle in water, 1 tsp at a time, stirring until dough forms.

3. Press about 3 Tbs of dough into each of 4 ungreased, 6-ounce custard cups, up to within $\frac{1}{2}$ inch of top.

4. Bake until golden brown, 10 to 12 minutes; let cool 10 minutes. Carefully remove pastries from cups with a small metal spatula; let cool completely on wire rack.

5. Fill each pastry cup with $\frac{1}{3}$ cup of yogurt; garnish with fresh fruit if desired.

*Source:* Recipe provided courtesy of Gold Medal® Flour.

Some of Juan's friends want to have dessert. Since the recipe on the left will only make enough yogurt cups for four people, Juan makes a chart to find the amounts of each ingredient he will need to serve more or fewer than four people.

| Servings | 4 | 2 | 8 | 6 | 10 | 16 |
|---|---|---|---|---|---|---|
| Flour (cups) | $\frac{3}{4}$ | | | | | |
| Margarine (cups) | $\frac{1}{4}$ | | | | | |
| Powdered Sugar (tablespoons) | 3 | | | | | |
| Water (teaspoons) | $2\frac{1}{2}$ | | | | | |
| Yogurt (cups) | $1\frac{1}{3}$ | | | | | |

8. Complete the table on **Student Activity Sheet 7** for the Yogurt Cups recipe.

9. There are different ways to find the amounts of ingredients for 10 servings. Describe two possibilities.

10. Is it possible to use containers other than cups and spoons to measure the ingredients for the yogurt cups recipe? Why or why not?

**8.**

| Servings | 4 | 2 | 8 | 6 | 10 | 16 |
|---|---|---|---|---|---|---|
| Flour (cups) | $\frac{3}{4}$ | $\frac{3}{8}$ | $1\frac{1}{2}$ | $1\frac{1}{8}$ | $1\frac{7}{8}$ | 3 |
| Margarine (cups) | $\frac{1}{4}$ | $\frac{1}{8}$ | $\frac{1}{2}$ | $\frac{3}{8}$ | $\frac{5}{8}$ | 1 |
| Powdered Sugar (tablespoons) | 3 | $1\frac{1}{2}$ | 6 | $4\frac{1}{2}$ | $7\frac{1}{2}$ | 12 |
| Water (teaspoons) | $2\frac{1}{2}$ | $1\frac{1}{4}$ | 5 | $3\frac{3}{4}$ | $6\frac{1}{4}$ | 10 |
| Yogurt (cups) | $1\frac{1}{3}$ | $\frac{2}{3}$ | $2\frac{2}{3}$ | 2 | $3\frac{1}{3}$ | $5\frac{1}{3}$ |

**9.** Answers will vary. Sample student responses:

Since two servings plus eight servings equals 10 servings, I can add the numbers in these two columns for each ingredient. For example, $\frac{3}{8}$ cup of flour for two servings plus $1\frac{1}{2}$ cups of flour for eight servings equals $1\frac{7}{8}$ cups of flour for 10 servings.

Since four servings plus six servings equals 10 servings, I can add the numbers in these two columns for each ingredient:

$\frac{3}{4}$ cups of flour $= \frac{6}{8}$ cups of flour

$\frac{6}{8}$ cup $+ \frac{9}{8}$ cup $= 1\frac{5}{8}$ cups, or $1\frac{7}{8}$ cups.

**10.** Yes, only the ratios between the ingredients matter. Therefore, if you want to vary the amount that the recipe makes, it is possible to use containers other than cups and spoons, as long as the ratios between the ingredients stay the same.

**Materials** Student Activity Sheet 7 (one per student); fraction strips, optional (one set per student); additional recipes, optional (one per student)

**Overview** Students again use ratio tables to determine the correct amounts of each ingredient in a recipe when the number of servings is changed.

**About the Mathematics** Although problems **7** and **8** are alike, students may have more difficulty with problem **8,** since it involves mixed numbers. The relative nature of fractions is addressed in problem **10**. Note that from a mathematical point of view, there is no fixed order for filling in the different columns in the table. Note, also, that the strategy of halving is used to complete the two servings column.

**Planning** Be sure that students have their fraction strips available. After students have worked on the ratio table for a short time, discuss how to fill in the second column since halving is probably a new strategy. You can also discuss which columns and rows students think are easy to complete and why. Then students may finish the problems on this page individually or in pairs. Discuss students' strategies for problems **9** and **10**.

**Comments about the Problems**

**8. Informal Assessment** This problem assesses students' ability to use informal strategies for operations with fractions and their understanding of and ability to use the relationships between benchmark fractions. Some students may need to make a separate ratio table for each ingredient. To keep track of their computations, students can write the strategies they use next to each table.

**9. Homework** This problem may be assigned as homework. Refer students to the strategies used in the examples on pages 17 and 18 of the Student Book.

**10.** Discuss the possibility of measuring the ingredients using larger containers, such as buckets, or smaller containers, such as spoons.

**Extension** If students have difficulty completing the problems above, you may want to provide additional recipes that they can use to determine the amounts of each ingredient as the number of servings changes.

# METRIC MEASURE

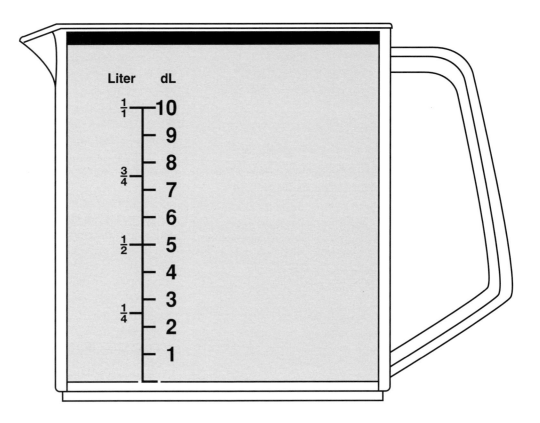

Above you see a picture of a measuring cup that is marked in liters and deciliters (dL).

**11.** How many deciliters are in one liter?

**12.** How many deciliters are in $\frac{1}{4}$ liter?

**13.** The measurements $\frac{1}{4}$ liter and $\frac{3}{4}$ liter are shown on the cup above. Why doesn't the drawing show $\frac{2}{4}$ liter?

**11.** 10 deciliters

**12.** $2\frac{1}{2}$ deciliters

**13.** because $\frac{2}{4}$ liter is the same as $\frac{1}{2}$ liter

**Materials** One-liter measuring cup, optional (one per class); fraction strips, optional (one set per student)

**Overview** Students discuss metric measurements of volume, specifically liters and deciliters. They relate deciliters to fractions like $\frac{1}{4}$ and $\frac{3}{4}$.

**About the Mathematics** The problems on this page and the next focus on the relationship between deciliters and fractions. Students are also informally introduced to the relationship between fractions and decimals. However, decimals are not explicitly studied in this unit. The relationship between fractions and decimals is discussed more extensively in the unit *Measure for Measure*. Note: In the picture on page 20 of the Student Book, one liter does not fill the entire measuring cup.

**Planning** You might briefly discuss what students already know about the metric system. It might be helpful to display a one-liter measuring cup. You can also discuss how liters relate to gallons (one liter equals approximately $\frac{1}{4}$ gallon). Students can work on problems **11–13** individually or in pairs. You can complete problems **11** through **16** during one class session.

**Comments about the Problems**

**11.** Students can answer this question by reading the measuring scale on the cup, but they must understand that $\frac{1}{1}$ liter is the same as 1 liter. You can discuss other fractions that can be used to label the upper mark on the measuring cup, such as $\frac{4}{4}$. This concept can also be discussed after problem **13.**

**12.** Students can answer this question by reading the measuring scale on the cup.

**13. Informal Assessment** This problem assesses students' ability to use equivalent forms of benchmark fractions within a context. The problem makes the equivalence of $\frac{2}{4}$ and $\frac{1}{2}$ explicit. If students are having difficulty, refer them to the fraction strips.

**Extension** You can discuss other fractions that can be used to label different measuring lines, such as eighths, twelfths, $\frac{3}{6}$ for $\frac{1}{2}$, and so forth. This activity can be assigned as homework and/or discussed in class.

**Did You Know?** A standard one cup (8 ounces) measuring cup equals about $\frac{1}{4}$ liter or $2\frac{1}{2}$ deciliters.

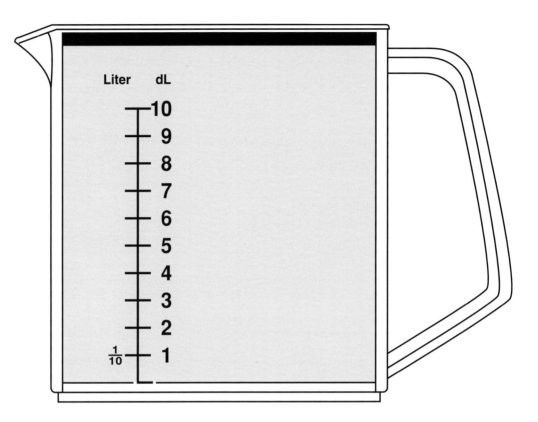

Here is another measuring cup.

**14. a.** What is the difference between the cup on page 20 and this cup?

**b.** On **Student Activity Sheet 8**, write the fractions of a liter that correspond to the measuring lines pictured above.

**15.** Draw measuring lines for $\frac{1}{3}$ liter and $\frac{2}{3}$ liter on the measuring cup on **Student Activity Sheet 8.**

**16.** How many deciliters are in $\frac{1}{3}$ liter?

**14. a.** The measuring cup on page 20 has measuring lines on the left in fourths. The measuring cup on page 21 has measuring lines on the left in tenths.

**b.**

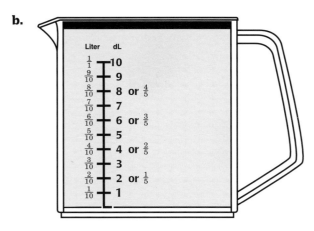

**15.**

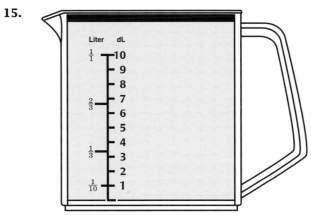

**16.** between 3 and 4 deciliters

**Materials** Student Activity Sheet 8 (one per student); fraction strip, optional (one set per student)

**Overview** Students write fractions (tenths) that correspond to the deciliters marked on a measuring cup. They also compare tenths to thirds.

**Planning** Students may work problems **14–16** individually or in pairs. These problems can also be assigned as homework and discussed the next day.

**Comments about the Problems**

**14. a. Homework** This problem may be assigned as homework. Suggest that students compare the measuring cup on Student Activity Sheet 8 to that shown on page 20 of the Student Book to see the differences between the two.

 **b. Informal Assessment** This problem assesses students' ability to recognize part-whole relationships. It may also be assigned as homework. If students are having difficulty, let them use fraction strips. For some of the measuring lines, there are at least two possible fractional answers, such as $\frac{2}{10}$ and $\frac{1}{5}$.

**15. Homework** This problem may be assigned as homework. Students do not have to measure precisely before drawing the lines. They can use the strategy from the fruit tape activity of dividing by folding into three equal parts.

**16. Homework** This problem may be assigned as homework. Students do not have to give an exact answer. An answer, such as "a little more than three deciliters" is appropriate.

**Extension** You may want to discuss why the metric system, which uses units of tenths, is more widely used throughout the world than the standard measuring system that uses units of halves, thirds, fourths, and so on. Students may suggest that it is easier to locate where three-tenths or seven-tenths is on a one-liter measuring cup than to find $\frac{3}{4}$ or $\frac{7}{8}$ on a standard measuring cup. Others may suggest that it is easier to use units of ten in computation rather than units of thirds or sixths.

# Summary

There are several ways to use the numbers in the columns of ratio tables to find the numbers in a new column.

Table 1
*Multiplying*

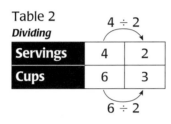

Table 3

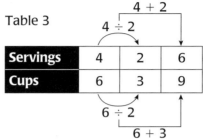

Table 2
*Dividing*

Table 4

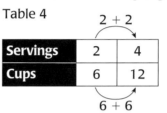

Often, it is useful to use a combination of methods.

Table 5

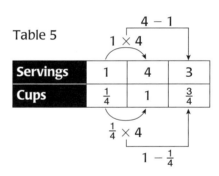

## Summary Questions

**17. a.** Table 1 uses multiplying, and Table 2 uses dividing. What operations do Tables 3 and 4 use?

    **b.** Find another way to produce the third column in Table 5.

**18.** Find a recipe for your favorite dish. Make a table to show the amounts of ingredients needed to make different numbers of servings.

**17. a.** Answers will vary. Sample student response:

Table 3 uses dividing and adding. Table 4 uses doubling.

**b.** Answers will vary. Sample student response:

I could multiply both numbers in the first column by three.

**18.** Answers will vary.

**Materials** additional recipes (one per student)

**Overview** Students read the Summary, which reviews different strategies that can be used with a ratio table to solve fraction and proportion problems. They analyze ratio tables to determine which operations were used to obtain specific numbers and make a ratio table showing the amounts of ingredients needed to make different numbers of servings.

**About the Mathematics** The ratio table reappears in many *Mathematics in Context* units. *Number Tools* includes a complete section on the ratio table and this model is extended in *Grasping Sizes* and other units in the number strand.

**Planning** You can have students read the Summary and complete problem **17.** Be sure to discuss students' solutions for this problem. Problem **18** can be assigned as homework and/or used for assessment. If students have difficulty with ratio tables, you may use the ratio table activities in *Number Tools* for extra practice. After students complete Section C, you may assign appropriate activities in the Try This! section, located on pages 38–41 of the Student Book, for homework.

**Comments about the Problems**

**17.** Table 3 shows two operations: column two is the result of dividing the numbers in column one by two, and column three is the result of adding the numbers in columns one and two. Table 4 shows doubling. Table 5 also shows two operations: column two is the result of multiplying column one by four, and column three is the result of multiplying the numbers in column one by three. Column three is also the result of taking $\frac{3}{4}$ of the numbers in column two (multiplying the numbers in column two by $\frac{3}{4}$).

**18. Informal Assessment** This problem assesses students' ability to solve context problems in which simple fractions are involved, using informal strategies, and their ability to use informal strategies for operations with fractions. You may also assign this problem as homework. Students should use recipes that include fractional quantities to provide them with additional opportunities to work with fractions.

## Work Students Do

The context of food recipes is used again in this section. Students complete a ratio table to determine the quantities of ingredients needed for a recipe if the number of servings decreases.

The context of dividing sausages and blocks of cheese gives students another opportunity to visualize concrete examples of part-whole relationships, but here the whole is an irregularly shaped object. Students also explore the relationship between weight and size. Given the weights of whole objects, students identify the parts that represent certain weights and estimate the weights of pieces being cut off. The concluding activities introduce students to the population bar, a visual representation used for part-whole comparisons. The population bar is similar to the *fraction bar* model that is introduced in the unit *Per Sense.*

## Goals

**Students will:**

- use fractions to describe part-whole relationships;
- estimate fractions and parts of wholes;
- develop an understanding of and use the relationships between benchmark fractions;*
- solve contextual problems in which simple fractions are involved, using informal strategies.

*Indicates a goal that may be assessed in other sections of this unit*

## Pacing

- approximately three 45-minute class sessions

## Vocabulary

- fraction bar

## About the Mathematics

The mathematical content of this section emphasizes the partitioning of various objects. The questions are designed to build on the ideas from the first three sections of the unit, including estimation and the relationships between benchmark fractions. These relationships, as well as the use of fractions as operators, are implicit elements of the sausage and cheese activity.

The *fraction bar* model is frequently used to visually represent part-whole comparisons of population and other types of data. This section's realistic contexts help to extend students' reasoning with fractional quantities.

## Materials

- Student Activity Sheets 9 and 10, pages 111–112 of the Teacher Guide (one of each per student)
- transparency of Student Activity Sheet 10, page 61 of the Teacher Guide, optional (one per class)
- copies of drawings on page 26 of the Student Book, optional (one per student)
- cereal or other food boxes, page 65 of the Teacher Guide (several per class)
- fraction strips, pages 59 and 67 of the Teacher Guide, optional (one set per student)
- rulers, page 65 of the Teacher Guide, optional (one per student)
- paper strips, pages 63, 65 and 67 of the Teacher Guide, optional (seven per student)
- population data from your class, school, town, or another source to make population (fraction) bars for problem 9, page 67 of the Teacher Guide

## Planning Instruction

To introduce this section, you may want to encourage students to bring in cookbooks from various countries and then compare the books' common units of measure. You may also ask students to look for a recipe at home in which fractions are involved and bring it to class.

To prepare for the activity on page 27 of the Student Book, you may want to ask students to bring in empty food boxes, such as cereal or rice boxes.

Students may work individually or in pairs on problems 1–4, 7–8, and 12–13. Students may work in pairs or in small groups on problems 5, 6, 10 and 11.

There are no optional problems in this section.

## Homework

Problems 2 (page 58 of the Teacher Guide), 3 (page 60 of the Teacher Guide), 8 (page 66 of the Teacher Guide), and 12 and 13 (page 70 of the Teacher Guide) can be assigned as homework. The Extensions (pages 59 and 71 of the Teacher Guide) and the Interdisciplinary Connection (page 67 of the Teacher Guide) can also be assigned as homework. After students complete Section D, you may assign appropriate activities from the Try This! section located on pages 38–41 of the *Some of the Parts* Student Book. The Try This! activities reinforce the key math concepts introduced in this section.

## Planning Assessment

- Problems 3, 4, and 13 can be used to informally assess students' ability to estimate fractions and parts of wholes.
- Problems 8–9 can be used to informally assess students' ability to use fractions to describe part-whole relationships and solve contextual problems in which simple fractions are involved, using informal strategies.
- Problem 12 can be used to informally assess students' ability to solve contextual problems in which simple fractions are involved, using informal strategies.

## D. HOW MUCH?

# Now You're Cooking

Here is a recipe for a dish that Eileen and her mother are planning to make for dinner.

## Chicken & Tortilla Casserole

*Makes 8 servings.*

### Ingredients

8 skinless, boneless chicken breast halves
1 lb jar of salsa (any will do, but green salsa is very spicy)
1 cup light sour cream
$\frac{1}{2}$ cup half-and-half
12 tortillas (blue corn, corn, or flour)
4 cups (1 lb) shredded cheddar cheese
$\frac{1}{3}$ cup grated Parmesan cheese

Preheat oven to 350°F.

Rinse chicken with cold water. Fill half of a five-quart saucepan with water. Bring to a boil. Turn off burner, carefully add chicken, and cover. After 20 minutes, check the chicken: place one piece on the cutting board, cut to center of thickest part. If chicken is still pink inside, return it to pan, cover, and let stand for 10 more minutes. Repeat. When chicken is no longer pink in the center, place all chicken on cutting board. Cut into bite-size pieces. Place half of the chicken in a 9″ × 13″ baking pan. Cover with half of the salsa.

Mix sour cream with half-and-half until well blended. Spoon half of the mixture over chicken and salsa.

Cut tortillas into one-inch wide strips. Top sour cream mixture with half of the tortilla strips and half of the cheddar cheese.

Repeat all layers using remaining ingredients. Cover pan with foil. Fold foil around edges of pan to seal. Bake 40 minutes.

Remove from oven. Carefully remove foil, starting on side away from you. (Steam can burn.) Sprinkle top of casserole with Parmesan cheese. Return pan to oven. Bake, uncovered, for about 5 more minutes, until cheese is golden brown. Remove pan from oven. Let casserole stand for 10 minutes before serving.

**Overview** Students read a recipe for chicken and tortilla casserole.

**About the Mathematics** As in Section C, students use ratio tables to find the amounts of ingredients if the number of servings in a recipe decreases.

**Planning** You might want to read the recipe aloud, explaining any ingredient that may be unfamiliar to students.

**Did You Know?** Corn meal (ground corn) is used to make the corn pancakes that are called tortillas. Tortillas are the basis for many Mexican and Central American specialties such as *enchiladas* (tortillas dipped in sauce and rolled around pork or chicken before baking), *tostadas* (fried tortillas covered with onions, chili peppers, grated cheese, meat, lettuce, tomatoes, avocados, and/or beans), and *quesadillas* (tortillas folded around meat, beans, cheese, or vegetables).

| | | |
|---|---|---|
| **Number of Servings** | 8 | |
| **Number of Chicken Breast Halves** | 8 | |
| **Jars of Salsa** | 1 | |
| **Cups of Light Sour Cream** | 1 | |
| **Cups of Half-and-Half** | $\frac{1}{2}$ | |
| **Number of Corn Tortillas** | 12 | |
| **Cups of Shredded Cheddar Cheese** | 4 | |
| **Cups of Grated Parmesan Cheese** | $\frac{1}{3}$ | |

Eileen and her mother are making dinner for themselves and two friends. The recipe for Chicken & Tortilla Casserole makes eight servings, but Eileen and her mother want to make the recipe for only four.

1. Use **Student Activity Sheet 9** to decide how much of each ingredient they will need.

A few months later it is Eileen's mother's birthday. Eileen decides to fix Chicken & Tortilla Casserole for her mother's birthday dinner.

2. Now Eileen is cooking dinner for only two people. How much will she need of each ingredient? You may extend your table from problem **1** if you wish.

**1.**

| Number of Servings | 8 | 4 |
|---|---|---|
| Number of Chicken Breast Halves | 8 | 4 |
| Jars of Salsa | 1 | $\frac{1}{2}$ |
| Cups of Light Sour Cream | 1 | $\frac{1}{2}$ |
| Cups of Half-and-Half | $\frac{1}{2}$ | $\frac{1}{4}$ |
| Number of Corn Tortillas | 12 | 6 |
| Cups of Shredded Cheddar Cheese | 4 | 2 |
| Cups of Grated Parmesan Cheese | $\frac{1}{3}$ | $\frac{1}{6}$ |

**2.**

| Number of Servings | 8 | 4 | 2 |
|---|---|---|---|
| Number of Chicken Breast Halves | 8 | 4 | 2 |
| Jars of Salsa | 1 | $\frac{1}{2}$ | $\frac{1}{4}$ |
| Cups of Light Sour Cream | 1 | $\frac{1}{2}$ | $\frac{1}{4}$ |
| Cups of Half-and-Half | $\frac{1}{2}$ | $\frac{1}{4}$ | $\frac{1}{8}$ |
| Number of Corn Tortillas | 12 | 6 | 3 |
| Cups of Shredded Cheddar Cheese | 4 | 2 | 1 |
| Cups of Grated Parmesan Cheese | $\frac{1}{3}$ | $\frac{1}{6}$ | $\frac{1}{12}$ |

**Materials** Student Activity Sheet 9 (one per student), fraction strips, optional (one set per student)

**Overview** Students complete a ratio table to determine the quantity of each ingredient needed for a recipe when the number of servings decreases.

**About the Mathematics** In this situation, students begin to informally divide fractions by two or to multiply fractions by one-half.

It is not important that students use formal notation such as $\frac{1}{2} \times \frac{1}{2} = \frac{1}{4}$. The primary goal is for students to find relationships between fractions, such as half of $\frac{1}{2}$ is $\frac{1}{4}$, half of $\frac{1}{3}$ is $\frac{1}{6}$, and half of $\frac{1}{4}$ is $\frac{1}{8}$. Students may use their fraction strips for visual support.

**Planning** Students can work individually or in pairs on problems **1** and **2.** Discuss these problems with the class.

**Comments about the Problems**

1. Some students may need to use their fraction strips. Have students explain what they did with the given numbers, so that the relationships between simple fractions can be emphasized. For example, students may explain that "half of $\frac{1}{2}$ cup is $\frac{1}{4}$ cup."

2. **Homework** This problem may be assigned as homework.

**Extension** You may ask students to write the relationships they discover between fractions. The same relationship may be expressed in different ways. For example: half of $\frac{1}{2}$ cup is $\frac{1}{4}$ cup; $\frac{1}{4}$ cup + $\frac{1}{4}$ cup = $\frac{1}{2}$ cup; $\frac{1}{2} \times \frac{1}{2} = \frac{1}{4}$. The last expression is the most formal. Do not require students to use this notation.

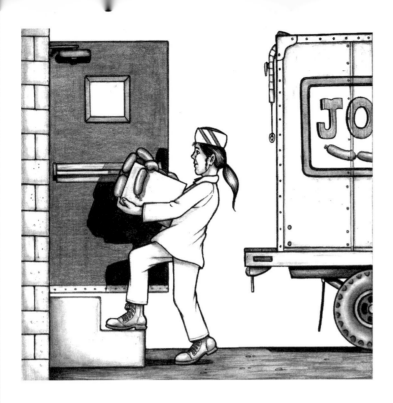

The school cafeteria staff buys large quantities of food for lunches. After receiving a food shipment, the cafeteria staff divides it into the amounts needed for recipes (just like Eileen divided the casserole ingredients).

**3.** Use **Student Activity Sheet 10** to draw lines and color the piece on each food item that is needed by the cafeteria staff.

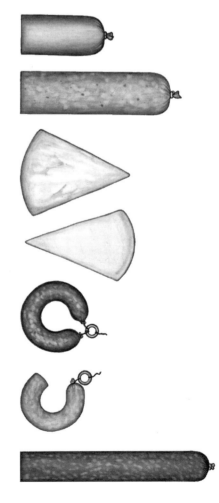

**a.** This piece of bologna weighs 400 grams. Cut off 100 grams.

**b.** This piece of salami weighs 600 grams. Cut off 450 grams.

**c.** This piece of cheese weighs 1,200 grams. Cut off 800 grams.

**d.** This piece of cheese weighs 1,600 grams. Cut off 1,200 grams.

**e.** This piece of sausage weighs 1,200 grams. Cut off 200 grams.

**f.** This piece of sausage weighs 900 grams. Cut off 100 grams.

**g.** This piece of pepperoni weighs 2,400 grams. Cut off 2,000 grams.

**3. a.** $\left(\frac{1}{4}\right)$

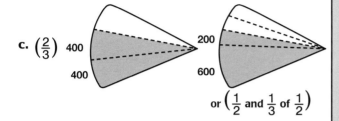

**b.** $\left(\frac{3}{4}\right)$

**c.** $\left(\frac{2}{3}\right)$ 400  200
400  600

or $\left(\frac{1}{2} \text{ and } \frac{1}{3} \text{ of } \frac{1}{2}\right)$

**d.** $\left(\frac{3}{4}\right)$

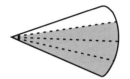

**e.** $\left(\frac{1}{6}\right)$ or $\left(\frac{1}{3} \text{ of } \frac{1}{2}\right)$

**f.** $\left(\frac{1}{9}\right)$

**g.** $\left(\frac{1}{2} \text{ and } \frac{1}{2} \text{ of } \frac{1}{2}\right.$
and $\left.\frac{1}{3} \text{ of } \frac{1}{2} \text{ of } \frac{1}{2}\right)$

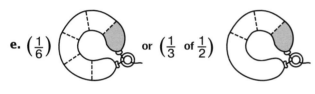

1200    600   200
$\left(\frac{1}{2}\right)$  $\left(\frac{1}{2} \text{ of } \frac{1}{2}\right)$

or $\left(\frac{1}{2} \text{ and } \frac{1}{4} \text{ and } \frac{1}{12}\right)$

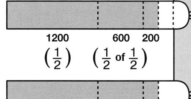

1200    600   200
$\left(\frac{1}{2}\right)$  $\left(\frac{1}{4}\right)\left(\frac{1}{12}\right)$

or $\left(\frac{10}{12}\right)$

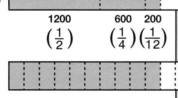

or $\left(\frac{5}{6}\right)$

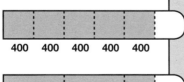

400  400  400  400  400

or $\left(\frac{2}{3} \text{ and } \frac{1}{2} \text{ of } \frac{1}{3}\right)$

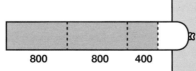

800    800   400

**Materials** Student Activity Sheet 10 (one per student); transparency of Student Activity Sheet 10, optional (one per class)

**Overview** Students divide sausages and blocks of cheese into equal pieces to obtain the correct weights needed for cafeteria recipes.

**About the Mathematics** The context of dividing sausages and blocks of cheese gives students the opportunity to visualize concrete examples of part-whole relationships. For example, to cut off a 200-gram section from a 1,200-gram sausage, students can first divide the sausage into two pieces, each weighing 600 grams. They can then divide one of these pieces into three parts, each weighing 200 grams. Students implicitly use fractions to make these partitions; they take $\frac{1}{3}$ of a $\frac{1}{2}$ piece. The drawing below shows that the result is $\frac{1}{6}$ of the whole:

**Planning** It may be helpful to display one or two copies of the sausages and blocks of cheese on a transparency. Students may work individually or in pairs on problem **3.** Be sure to discuss this problem with the class. It may be assigned as homework and/or used as assessment.

**Comments about the Problems**

3. **Informal Assessment** This problem assesses students' ability to estimate fractions and parts of wholes.

   Students may find this problem easier to solve if they draw auxiliary lines. It may be helpful for some students to make paper models of the sausages and blocks of cheese so that they can fold them along the appropriate lines. Allow students to solve the problem using their own strategies. The relationship between division and fractions can be emphasized by asking: *What fraction describes the part that has been cut off?*

   Also discuss the relationships between fractions, such as half of $\frac{1}{2}$ is $\frac{1}{4}$. This problem may also be assigned as homework.

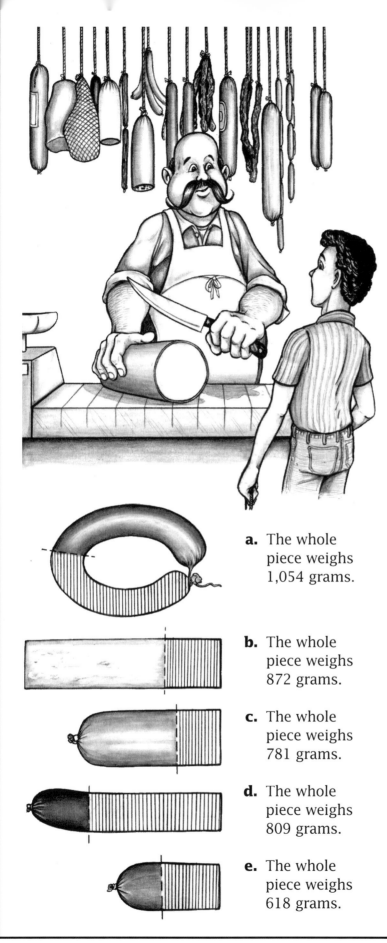

In the last set of problems, the weights of the pieces of meat and cheese were rounded to the nearest 100 or 50 grams. If you weigh a piece of meat on an electronic balance, the weight could be rounded to the nearest gram.

Abe is shopping at a market where they sell food that is not yet packaged. Abe goes to a stand and asks, "May I have 200 grams of bologna?" The butcher takes the piece of bologna from the case and weighs it. The scale indicates that the piece weighs 623 grams. The butcher thinks, "I need about one-third of it."

Before cutting, the butcher shows Abe the piece that is going to be cut off and asks, "Do you want a piece about this size?" Abe agrees that the piece is about the right size, so it is cut, and Abe buys the bologna.

**a.** The whole piece weighs 1,054 grams.

**b.** The whole piece weighs 872 grams.

**c.** The whole piece weighs 781 grams.

**d.** The whole piece weighs 809 grams.

**e.** The whole piece weighs 618 grams.

**4.** On the left you see some pieces of sausage and cheese. The dotted lines indicate where the butcher will cut. Estimate how much the cutoff piece (the part with the vertical lines) will weigh.

## Solutions and Samples
*of student work*

4. Answers will vary. Sample responses:

   a. about half of the whole, so about 500 grams

   b. about one-fourth of the whole, so about 220 grams

   c. about one-third of the whole, so about 250 grams

   d. about three-fourths of the whole, so about 600 grams

   e. about two-thirds of the whole, so about 400 grams

## Hints and Comments

**Materials** Copies of drawings on page 26 of the Student Book, optional (one per student); paper strips, optional (five per student)

**Overview** Given the weight of a whole piece of sausage or cheese, students estimate the weight of a section that will be cut off.

**About the Mathematics** Problem 4 reinforces the relationship between fractions and division. For example, in problem **4a** one-half of the sausage is to be cut. To find the weight of one-half of the sausage, students must divide by two. This problem is related to problems **1** and **3** of Section B, in which students used fractions to describe how much milk was in a tin can. Now students are asked to find a fractional part and to relate that part to a weight. Again, students informally use a fraction as an operator.

**Planning** It may be helpful to prepare extra copies of the drawings on page 26 of the Student Book for students who may want to draw auxiliary lines in each picture. Students may also use paper strips. Students can work individually or in pairs on problem **4.** Discuss this problem with the whole class, so that students can share their strategies.

**Comments about the Problems**

4. **Informal Assessment** This problem assesses students' ability to estimate fractions and parts of wholes.

   First, students determine what part (fraction) of piece of sausage or cheese will be cut off. Then, they should round the given number of total grams in order to estimate the weight of the part that is being cut off.

   Students' answers may vary depending on how they estimate and/or round the cut-off part. This discrepancy is not important if students can explain their reasoning. For example, in problem **4d,** some students may find that the cut-off section is about two-thirds of the whole, while others may determine that it is about three-fourths of the whole.

A full box of the cornflakes pictured on the right weighs 12 ounces.

**5.** What if some of the cornflakes have been eaten? Do you have to weigh the box to know the weight of what is left? Find another way to make an estimate.

# Activity

Collect some boxes of food, such as flour, cereal, rice, and so on. The boxes may be full or empty. Mark the beginning level (real or made-up) of the food on the outside of the box. Use another color to draw in some lines that may help you estimate the weights of different levels of food. You may want to draw in quarters, thirds, or other divisions. Label each line with the fraction it represents. Now label each line again, this time with the weight represented by that line.

**6. a.** How much would food at each of the levels you marked weigh? How do you know?

**b.** Why did you choose the fractions you did?

**c.** Do you think now that you chose the best fractions for your lines? Why or why not?

## Solutions and Samples
*of student work*

**5.** Answers will vary. Some students may respond that you need to weigh the cereal box to determine the weight of the cereal that is left. Other students may suggest that you could visually estimate what fraction of the cornflakes is left and take that fraction of the total weight.

**6. a–c.** Answers will vary.

## Hints and Comments

**Materials** cereal or other food boxes (several per class); rulers or paper strips, optional (one per student)

**Overview** Students use fractions to estimate the weight of the contents of a box of food.

**About the Mathematics** This problem is related to problem **5** in Section B, in which students marked measuring lines on cans to show halves, thirds, fourths, sixths, eighths and twelfths. In this context, they not only use fractions to describe different parts of a whole; they also relate the fractional parts to weight. Students mark a double number line on the boxes they use for this activity, displaying both fractions and their corresponding weights.

Again, students informally use fractions as operators. For example, to find the weight that corresponds to $\frac{1}{3}$ of the box, students divide the total weight by three. To find $\frac{2}{3}$ of the box's weight, they can double the weight of $\frac{1}{3}$ of the box.

**Planning** After students have finished problem **5,** you may want to discuss the problem briefly with the class. Then have students continue with problem **6.** Students may work in pairs or in small groups on these problems.

### Comments about the Problems

**5.** Some students may mention that boxes of cereal are not always filled to the top. Discuss how to handle this fact. Students may suggest marking the level of the box when it is full or, in other words, indicating the level that would be the "whole." You can ignore this fact because estimating is more important than exact calculations.

**6.** Allow students to decide how precise they want their answers to be. Since the measuring lines should be used only for estimating, a rough division of the height into four (or three or six) equal pieces is sufficient. However, students may use paper strips or rulers.

Observe whether or not students draw the lines by sight. If so, ask them how they are dividing the whole into equal parts. Some students may divide the whole into eight equal pieces by drawing one line for $\frac{1}{8}$, another for $\frac{2}{8}$, and so on. However, the last piece may be too small or too large. A better approach is to begin with $\frac{1}{2}$ and use the relationships among $\frac{1}{2}$, $\frac{1}{4}$, and $\frac{1}{8}$; $\frac{1}{4}$ is half of a half, and $\frac{1}{8}$ is half of a half of a half.

# Populations and *Places*

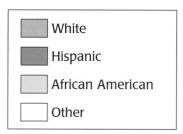

| | |
|---|---|
| ▨ | White |
| ▨ | Hispanic |
| ▨ | African American |
| ☐ | Other |

Most towns have people of different cultures. Below you see a diagram of one town's population. This kind of diagram is based on a fraction bar and can be called a *population bar*.

**7.** Use fractions to describe the cultural makeup of this town.

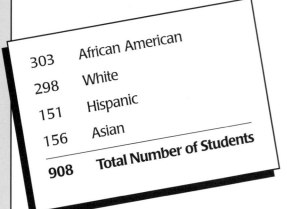

A group of students decided to make a population bar to show the population of their school. You can see the numbers they found on the left.

| | |
|---|---|
| 303 | African American |
| 298 | White |
| 151 | Hispanic |
| 156 | Asian |
| **908** | **Total Number of Students** |

**8. a.** Make a population bar for the school. Remember to add a key, explaining what each part stands for. You do not have to be precise.

**b.** Use your population bar to write fractions that describe the cultural makeup of the school.

## Activity

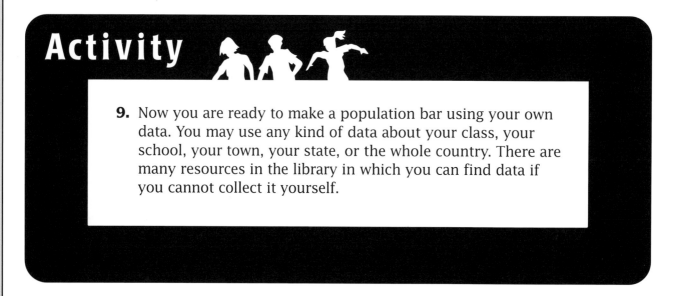

**9.** Now you are ready to make a population bar using your own data. You may use any kind of data about your class, your school, your town, your state, or the whole country. There are many resources in the library in which you can find data if you cannot collect it yourself.

**7.** About $\frac{1}{2}$ of the inhabitants are White; about $\frac{1}{4}$ are Hispanic; about $\frac{1}{8}$ are African-American; and about $\frac{1}{8}$ are from other cultures.

**8. a.**

☐ **African-American**

☐ **White**

☐ **Hispanic**

☐ **Asian**

**b.** In this school, about $\frac{1}{3}$ of the students are African-American; about $\frac{1}{3}$ are White; about $\frac{1}{6}$ are Hispanic; and about $\frac{1}{6}$ are Asian.

**9.** Students' population bars will vary, depending on the data collected.

**Materials** population data from your class, school, town, or another source; paper strips, optional (one per student)

**Overview** Students read a fraction bar (called a population bar in this context) and use fractions to estimate and describe a town's cultural makeup.

**About the Mathematics** Fractions are often used for part-whole comparisons. The population bar is a visual representation of this type of comparison. The "whole" in problem **7** is the population of the entire town.

**Planning** Decide in advance how you want to organize and arrange the activity in problem **9**. Students can work on the other problems in pairs or individually. You may decide to assign problem **8** as homework and/or use it for assessment.

**Comments about the Problems**

**7.** Students can use paper strips to find the fractions by folding.

**8–9. Informal Assessment** These problems assess students' ability to use fractions to describe part-whole relationships and solve contextual problems in which simple fractions are involved, using informal strategies.

Students should not aim for absolute precision when drawing the population bars. In this context, fraction bars are used to describe general preferences or facts.

**8.** Students can use different strategies to draw the population bar. They can draw the whole bar and then look for appropriate divisions. Another, easier strategy is to begin by drawing the part that represents the African-American population and then using this part to construct the other parts. The White population's section should be about the same size as the African-American section, and the parts of the other two about half the size of the African-American section.

**Interdisciplinary Connection** The context of these problems provides an opportunity for a social studies connection. You may wish to ask a social studies teacher to help students collect data for the activity in problem **9**.

Sullivanville was founded by Irish settlers. Today this is still obvious in the many Irish names in the town. Some students counted the Irish names in the class lists of two different middle schools in the town. These are the results:

Robert Fulton School:　206　Irish names (school population: 806 students)

Jane Hull School:　　　98　Irish names (school population: 305 students)

**10.** Which school has more students with Irish names? Explain your answer.

**The Main Street Plaza**

**The Commodore Building**

People have different reactions to the new Main Street Plaza. One well-known architect said she thinks it is ugly and too different from the style of the rest of the buildings on Main Street.

However, the newspaper's opinion poll reveals that $\frac{2}{3}$ of the citizens like the look of the Main Street Plaza. Asked for their opinion about the Commodore building on Main Street, five out of eight people say that they like it.

**11.** In the newspaper clipping above, you read what people think about two new buildings in a town, the Main Street Plaza and the Commodore building. Which of the two buildings do more people like? Explain your answer.

**10.** This question is deliberately ambiguous. Comparing only the numbers of students with Irish names in both schools, Fulton School has more students with Irish names. Comparing the ratios of students with Irish names to the total school populations, Jane Hull School has a higher proportion of students with Irish names. Students who compare the two quantities in a relative way (using ratios) may make a drawing like the one below to defend their interpretation:

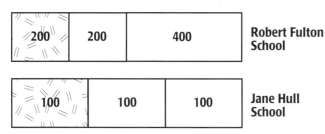

**11.** The Main Street Plaza

Explanations will vary. Sample student responses:

The article does not give the number of people who responded to the survey, so I chose a number that can be divided by both three and eight. Suppose there were 24 people; $\frac{2}{3} = \frac{16}{24}$ and $\frac{5}{8} = \frac{15}{24}$. Since $\frac{16}{24}$ is larger than $\frac{15}{24}$, more people like the Main Street Plaza.

Five out of eight can be read as $\frac{5}{8}$. I used fraction strips to compare the fractions $\frac{2}{3}$ and $\frac{5}{8}$. Since $\frac{2}{3}$ is larger than $\frac{5}{8}$, more people like the Main Street Plaza.

**Overview** Students make part-whole comparisons with whole numbers, fractions, and ratios.

**About the Mathematics** Absolute comparisons can be made by looking only at numbers; relative comparisons can be made by looking at numbers in relation to other numbers. Fractions, ratios, and percents can be used to express relative comparisons.

In this unit, students begin to understand relative comparisons by using fractions and/or fraction bars. This concept is further emphasized in the unit *Per Sense,* in which students use percents to make relative comparisons. It is also addressed in the grade 6/7 unit *Smooth Operators,* in which ratios are discussed in relation to percents, fractions, and decimals.

**Planning** Students may work in pairs or in small groups on problems **10** and **11.** Be sure to discuss problem **10** with the whole class.

### Comments about the Problems

**10.** Accept both interpretations of the question as correct, but discuss the difference in interpretation with the whole class. If students choose the larger number of Irish names, encourage them to make a comparison based on the total number of students in each school.

Students may use population bars to find the fraction of Irish students in each school. Their solutions will most likely be $\frac{1}{4}$ Irish for the Robert Fulton School and $\frac{1}{3}$ Irish for the Jane Hull School. Students can then compare these two fractions. Some students may want to compare their population bars without using fractions; if so, they must draw rectangles of the same size for the two population bars. Note that this is not necessary if they use the bars only to find the fractions.

**11.** This problem illustrates how fractions are used in newspapers. *Half of, two thirds of,* and *three quarters of* are expressions that are often used. When these simple fractions cannot be used, newspapers use ratios *(five out of eight)* or percents, rather than fractions.

It is common to have fractions, ratios, and percents appear in the same article. Do not mention percents yet; this is the subject of the unit *Per Sense.* The fraction and ratio used in this press clipping make the problem rather difficult. You may wish to use it as an extra challenge problem.

# Summary

In this section you:

- reduced the number of servings of food by halving a recipe,

- showed how much meat or cheese would be cut off of a whole piece, knowing the total weight and the weight of the amount to be cut off,

- used population bars to describe the cultural makeup of towns.

## Summary Questions

**12.** How are the problems in this section related to the concept of fractions?

**13. a.** If the large bar of chocolate below weighs 95 kilograms, about how much does the shaded part weigh?

**b.** Explain how you found the weight of the shaded part of chocolate.

## Solutions and Samples
*of student work*

12. Answers will vary. One line of reasoning may be that you needed to use fractions or reason with fractions to solve the problems.

13. **a.** Estimates will vary. Sample estimates: about 30–32 kilograms, or more than 30 kilograms.

    **b.** Explanations will vary. Sample student explanation:

    I saw that I could divide the bar into three equal pieces and that the shaded part makes up about one-third of the bar. So I divided 95 kilograms by three. I rounded my answer to 32 kilograms.

## Hints and Comments

**Overview** Students read the Summary and solve problems related to the main concepts of the section.

**Planning** Have students read the Summary and work on problems **12** and **13** individually or in pairs. You may decide to use these problems as assessments or assign them as homework. After students complete Section D, you may assign appropriate activities in the Try This! section, located on pages 38–41 of the Student Book, for homework.

**Comments about the Problems**

12. **Informal Assessment** This problem assesses students' ability to solve contextual problems in which simple fractions are involved, using informal strategies. The problem can also be assigned as homework.

13. **Informal Assessment** This problem assesses students' ability to estimate fractions and parts of wholes. The problem may also be assigned as homework.

**Extension** You may ask students to create problems similar to those mentioned in the Summary. Also, ask students to show or explain how to use fractions to solve these problems. If they work in groups of three, they can each choose one of the topics mentioned in the Summary. After they have designed their own problems, they can exchange and solve their partners' problems.

## Work Students Do

In this section, a 36-kilometer race and a Literacy Run provide contexts for students to use informal strategies to order, compare, multiply, and divide fractions to determine distances. Students also work with fractions to convert city blocks to miles and vice versa. For the final problems in this section, students revisit Section A's first context: dividing a submarine sandwich into pieces.

## Goals

**Students will:**

- use informal strategies for operations with fractions;
- use equivalent forms of benchmark fractions within a context;
- order and compare fractions within a context;
- solve contextual problems in which simple fractions are involved, using informal strategies.

## Pacing

- approximately three 45-minute class sessions

## About the Mathematics

Ordering and locating fractions on a number line help students to think about fractions as measures (of distance). The notion of *unit of measure* is also important, and students use the relationship between city blocks and miles to solve problems involving fractions.

The double number line and the ratio table are used as models to help students understand the relationship between two numbers. Although these two models involve similar calculation methods, the double number line maintains the sequential order of the numbers, while the ratio table does not. For example, the following double number line and ratio table show the distance in miles of eight city blocks:

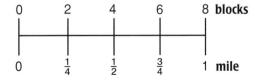

| Blocks | 4 | 2 | 6 | 8 |
|--------|---|---|---|---|
| Miles | $\frac{1}{2}$ | $\frac{1}{4}$ | $\frac{3}{4}$ | 1 |

## Materials

- Student Activity Sheets 11 and 12, pages 113 and 114 of the Teacher Guide (one of each per student)
- string or yarn, page 75 of the Teacher Guide (about one foot per student)
- rulers, page 75 of the Teacher Guide, optional (one per student)
- paper strips, pages 77 and 79 of the Teacher Guide, optional (two per student)
- fraction strips, page 75 of the Teacher Guide, optional (one set per student)
- transparency of the map on page 32 of the Student Book, page 77 of the Teacher Guide, optional (one per class)
- overhead projector, page 77 of the Teacher Guide, optional (one per class)

## Planning Instruction

Problem 1 is the first in this unit that explicitly asks students to order fractions. If they have difficulty ordering fractions, encourage students to use strips of paper to make comparisons.

Students can work in pairs or in small groups on problems 1–18 and individually or in pairs on problems 19 and 20. There are no optional problems in this section.

## Homework

Problems 8 and 9 (page 78 of the Teacher Guide), 14–18 (page 84 of the Teacher Guide), and the Extension (page 85 of the Teacher Guide) can be assigned as homework. After students complete Section E, you may assign appropriate activities from the Try This! section located on pages 38–41 of the *Some of the Parts* Student Book. The Try This! activities reinforce the key math concepts introduced in this section.

## Planning Assessment

- Problems 11, 14, and 15 can be used to informally assesses students' ability to use informal strategies for operations with fractions.
- Problem 12 can be used to informally assess students' ability to use equivalent forms of benchmark fractions and to order and compare fractions within a context.
- Problems 19 and 20 can be used to informally assess students' ability to solve contextual problems in which simple fractions are involved, using informal strategies.

# E. HOW FAR?

# The Great Race

Cedarberg and Poplarville have an annual race on the highway that connects the two towns. The total length of the race is 36 kilometers. The Cedarberg Middle School track team will organize the water stations along the length of the race. One team member will work at each station.

| Station | Team Member | Distance from Start |
|---------|-------------|---------------------|
| A | Cassie | $\frac{1}{3}$ |
| B | Jami | $\frac{2}{3}$ |
| C | J.R. | $\frac{1}{2}$ |
| D | Scott | $\frac{3}{4}$ |
| E | Lou | $\frac{1}{4}$ |

1. As the runners compete, which station will they come to first? Which will be second, third, and so on?

The students not assigned to work at the water stations are making a map to advertise the race, show the route, and indicate the locations of the water stations. To begin, they copy a map of the highway between the two towns. Then they decorate the map with some drawings.

2. Complete the map on **Student Activity Sheet 11** for the students by showing where the water stations will be.

1. The runners will arrive at the stations in the following order:
Station E, Station A, Station C, Station B, and Station D.

   • Some students may reason in the following manner:

   We know that $\frac{3}{4}$ and $\frac{2}{3}$ are both larger than $\frac{1}{2}$, $\frac{1}{3}$, and $\frac{2}{4}$. The fraction $\frac{3}{4}$ is $\frac{1}{4}$ away from one whole, and $\frac{2}{3}$ is $\frac{1}{3}$ away from one whole. Since $\frac{1}{4}$ is smaller than $\frac{1}{3}$, $\frac{3}{4}$ is closer to one than $\frac{2}{3}$. So, $\frac{3}{4}$ is the largest fraction, and $\frac{2}{3}$ is the next largest. The remaining fractions can be ordered from largest to smallest as $\frac{1}{2}$, $\frac{1}{3}$, and $\frac{1}{4}$.

   • Other students may compare the numbers of miles that the fractions represent:

   Half of 36 is 18; $\frac{1}{3}$ of 36 is 12; and $\frac{1}{4}$ of 36 is 9. So, $\frac{1}{2}$ is larger than $\frac{1}{3}$, and $\frac{1}{3}$ is larger than $\frac{1}{4}$. Two-thirds would be $12 \times 2$ (or 24) and $\frac{3}{4}$ would be $3 \times 9$ (or 27). This means that $\frac{3}{4}$ is larger than $\frac{2}{3}$.

2.

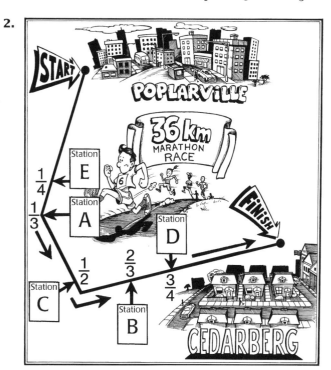

**Materials** Student Activity Sheet 11 (one per student); string or yarn (about one foot per student); rulers, optional (one per student); fraction strips, optional (one set per student)

**Overview** Students compare and order fractions and use them to locate the water stations along a racecourse.

**About the Mathematics** This race route is similar to a number line. The number line model helps students develop a conceptual understanding of fractions as numbers. Problem **1** is the first problem in this unit that explicitly asks students to order fractions. There are three main strategies that students can use to compare and order the given fractions:

• finding the fractions on fraction strips and comparing them,

• reasoning with fractions by using the relationships between the given fractions, and

• multiplying the given fractions by the total distance (36 kilometers) to compare the relative distance of each fractional part of the racecourse. This final strategy helps students develop a conceptual understanding of operations with fractions.

**Planning** Students can work in pairs or in small groups on these problems. Briefly discuss students' strategies for problem **1.**

### Comments about the Problems

1. Do not allow students to use the map on Student Book page 31 to answer this question. Instead, give them an opportunity to simply compare and order the fractions. Students may reason at different levels and in different ways, so be sure that they explain their answers.

2. If students are having difficulty, encourage them to use a piece of string or yarn and a ruler to find the location of the water stations.

# *Traveling to* SCHOOL

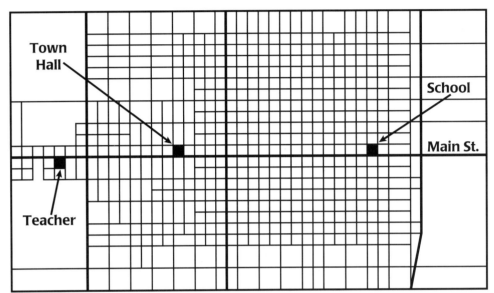

The city blocks in Cedarberg are $\frac{1}{8}$ of a mile long. Every morning, Belinda bikes the $1\frac{1}{2}$ miles from her home to school.

Sylvia lives only $\frac{1}{4}$ of a mile from school, so she walks there.

**3.** How many city blocks does Sylvia have to walk to get to school? How do you know?

**4.** How many city blocks does Belinda have to bike to get from her home to school? How did you figure it out?

**5.** Locate on the city map on **Student Activity Sheet 12** where Belinda and Sylvia could live.

**3.** Two blocks. Some students may reason in the following manner:

One mile is eight blocks. One-half of a mile is four blocks. Half of one-half of a mile is two blocks, so one-fourth of a mile equals two blocks.

Other students may use this reasoning:

Since one-fourth of a mile is twice as long as one-eighth of a mile, she walks two blocks.

**4.** Twelve blocks. Some students may reason in the following manner:

There are eight blocks in one mile and four blocks in $\frac{1}{2}$ of a mile, so the answer is $8+4$, or 12 blocks.

**5.** Answers will vary. Two possible answers follow.

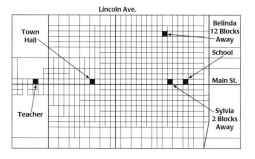

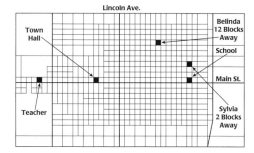

**Materials** Student Activity Sheet 12 (one per student); transparency of the map on page 32 of the Student Book, optional (one per class); paper strips, optional (one per student); overhead projector, optional (one per class)

**Overview** On the previous page, fractions were parts of the *whole* distance of the racecourse. In the context on this page, fractions are related to the *whole* distance of one mile. Given the information that one city block is $\frac{1}{8}$ of a mile, students express distances in miles as distances in city blocks.

**About the Mathematics** Students use their understanding of the relationships between fractions to solve these problems. They may informally operate with fractions using repeated addition: $\frac{1}{8}$ of a mile $+\frac{1}{8}$ of a mile $= \frac{1}{4}$ of a mile. They may also multiply: $2 \times \frac{1}{8}$ of a mile $= \frac{1}{4}$ of a mile.

**Planning** It may be helpful to make a transparency of the map on page 32 of the Student Book so that students can show their solutions and strategies on the overhead. Students may work on problems **3–5** in pairs or in small groups. You may want to discuss their strategies and answers to problems **3** and **4** as a class before having them work on problem **5** in pairs or in small groups.

**Comments about the Problems**

**3–4.** Observe how students determine their answers, noting which students use more formal notations. Students can reason using the relationships between fractions to solve these problems. If they are having difficulty, suggest that they make and use a fraction strip. Then students should consider what represents the whole and how the parts are related to the number of blocks. This strategy may lead to the creation of a double number line:

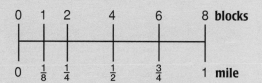

Mihn lives 13 blocks from school, at the corner of Lincoln Avenue and Main Street.

**6.** How many miles does Mihn live from school? Explain how you know.

Michael lives in the same block as the Town Hall, which is 17 blocks west of the school.

**7.** How many miles does Michael have to travel to get to school? How did you figure it out?

As you can see on the city map, a teacher lives on the far west side of Cedarberg. Her home is $3\frac{1}{2}$ miles from school.

**8.** How many city blocks does she live from school?

**9. a.** How many city blocks are there in 5 miles?

**b.** How many city blocks are there in $2\frac{1}{4}$ miles?

6. Mihn lives $1\frac{5}{8}$ miles from school.
   Possible explanation:

   There are eight blocks in one mile. One block is one-eighth of a mile. So five blocks are five-eighths of a mile; $1 + \frac{5}{8} = 1\frac{5}{8}$ miles.

7. Michael travels $2\frac{1}{8}$ miles. Possible explanation:
   $17 \times \frac{1}{8} = \frac{17}{8} = 2\frac{1}{8}$ miles

8. Twenty-eight blocks. Some students may reason in the following manner:

   One mile is eight blocks, and $3\frac{1}{2}$ miles is $3\frac{1}{2}$ times as long as one mile. Then you can figure that $3 \times 8$ blocks (or 24 blocks) plus $\frac{1}{2}$ of eight blocks (or four blocks) equals 28 blocks.

9. a. 40 blocks

   b. 18 blocks

**Materials** Student Activity Sheet 12 (one per student); paper strips, optional (one per student)

**Overview** Students convert distances in city blocks to distances in miles and vice versa.

**About the Mathematics** Some students may solve these problems using the strategy of repeated addition ($\frac{1}{4} + \frac{1}{4} + \frac{1}{4}$). Others may simply multiply to find a solution ($3 \times \frac{1}{4}$). Students may also develop and use their own informal strategies. Do not require that students use formal fraction notation at this point.

**Planning** Students should now know that five $\frac{1}{8}$ parts of a mile can be written as $\frac{5}{8}$ of a mile. If not, remind them about Section B, in which they labeled fractions on tin cans. Ask them what $\frac{2}{3}$ of a can means. Students can work in pairs or in small groups on problems **6–9.** You may assign problems **8** and **9** as homework.

**Comments about the Problems**

**6–7.** If students are having difficulty with these problems you can ask: *Will the distance be more or less than one mile?* [more than one mile] *How do you know?* [Eight blocks is one mile. So 13 blocks is definitely more than one mile.] You can also remind students to make and use drawings and fraction strips to solve the problems.

**8.** **Homework** This problem may be assigned as homework. If students start counting the blocks in the drawing, ask them if they can find another way to solve this problem.

**9.** **Homework** This problem may be assigned as homework. Encourage students to read the problem carefully to avoid mixing up the number of miles and the number of blocks as they convert from one unit to the other.

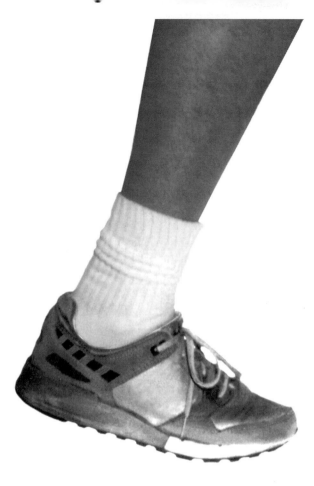

# Literacy *RUN*

The track team had so much fun working together for the Cedarberg–Poplarville run, they decided to organize another run to raise money for the local literacy group. They decide to run a stretch of $1\frac{1}{8}$ miles along Main Street.

Below you see an enlargement of the map of Main Street. The run will begin at the Town Hall.

**10.** Mark the turnaround point for the run on **Student Activity Sheet 12.**

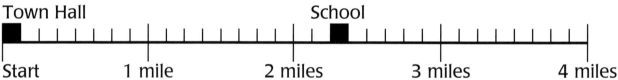

All of the kids in Cedarberg are invited to participate in the Literacy Run. They may run as many stretches as they wish. A stretch is either from the Town Hall to the turnaround point or from the turnaround point back to the Town Hall. Jami, for instance, wants to run five stretches:

Town Hall — turnaround — Town Hall — turnaround — Town Hall — turnaround

or $5 \times 1\frac{1}{8}$ miles.

**10.**

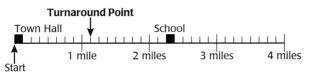

**Materials** Student Activity Sheet 12 (one per student)

**Overview** Students locate the turnaround point ($1\frac{1}{8}$ miles from the start) of a racecourse on a linear map that resembles a number line.

**About the Mathematics** On this page, it is made explicit that five stretches of $1\frac{1}{8}$ mile can be written as $5 \times 1\frac{1}{8}$. To check whether or not students understand the meaning of the notation $5 \times 1\frac{1}{8}$ miles, you can ask them to explain what $3 \times 1\frac{1}{8}$ miles means.

**Planning** Have a short class discussion about this page when students have finished reading the text. Students can work in pairs or in small groups on problem **10.**

**Comments about the Problems**

**10.** Some students may identify an incorrect location for the turnaround point because they used an incorrect starting point.

**11.** Here is a list of some of the kids from Cedarberg, with the number of stretches they intend to run. Copy this table into your notebook. Find how many miles each of them is going to run.

**Balaji** . . . . 2    stretches . . . . . $2 \times 1\frac{1}{8}$ = __?__ miles
**Meg**   . . . . 4    stretches . . . . . __?__ = __?__ miles
**Jami** . . . . . 5    stretches . . . . . __?__ = __?__ miles
**Julia**   . . . . 3    stretches . . . . . __?__ = __?__ miles
**Mary** . . . . 8    stretches . . . . . __?__ = __?__ miles
**Rodolfo** . . 6    stretches . . . . . __?__ = __?__ miles

Some people prefer to write $2\frac{2}{8}$ miles as $2\frac{1}{4}$ miles.

**12. a.** Why are $2\frac{2}{8}$ miles and $2\frac{1}{4}$ miles the same distance?

**b.** Look at your answers to problem **11.** Is it possible to write any of them in a different way without changing their meaning? If so, provide two examples.

**13. a.** Copy the ratio table below into your notebook and fill it in.

**b.** Rodolfo plans to run 10 stretches. How can he use the ratio table below to find out how many miles he will be running?

| Stretches | 1 | 2 | 3 | 4 | | | | |
|---|---|---|---|---|---|---|---|---|
| Miles | $1\frac{1}{8}$ | | | | | | | |

**11.** Balaji: $2\frac{1}{4}$ miles

Meg: $4\frac{1}{2}$ miles

Jami: $5\frac{5}{8}$ miles

Julia: $3\frac{3}{8}$ miles

Mary: 9 miles

Rodolfo: $6\frac{6}{8}$ or $6\frac{3}{4}$ miles

**12. a.** Answers will vary. Possible student response:

I know that $\frac{2}{8} = \frac{1}{4}$, so $2\frac{2}{8}$ must equal $2\frac{1}{4}$ miles.

**b.** Yes. Answers will vary. Sample answers:

$2\frac{2}{8}$ miles $= 2\frac{1}{4}$ miles

$4\frac{4}{8}$ miles $= 4\frac{1}{2}$ miles

$8\frac{8}{8}$ miles $= 9$ miles

$6\frac{6}{8}$ miles $= 6\frac{3}{4}$ miles

**13. a.**

| Stretches | 1 | 2 | 3 | 4 | 10 |
|---|---|---|---|---|---|
| Miles | $1\frac{1}{8}$ | $2\frac{1}{4}$ | $3\frac{3}{8}$ | $4\frac{1}{2}$ | $11\frac{1}{4}$ |

**b.**

| Stretches | 1 | 2 | 3 | 4 | 8 | 10 |
|---|---|---|---|---|---|---|
| Miles | $1\frac{1}{8}$ | $2\frac{1}{4}$ | $3\frac{3}{8}$ | $4\frac{1}{2}$ | 9 | $11\frac{1}{4}$ |

**or**

| Stretches | 1 | 2 | 3 | 4 | 5 | 10 |
|---|---|---|---|---|---|---|
| Miles | $1\frac{1}{8}$ | $2\frac{1}{4}$ | $3\frac{3}{8}$ | $4\frac{1}{2}$ | $5\frac{5}{8}$ | $11\frac{1}{4}$ |

**Overview** Students use informal strategies involving fraction operations to convert distances in miles to a certain number of stretches. They also use a ratio table to convert stretches to miles.

**About the Mathematics** The Literacy Run context used here is similar to the Traveling to School context from page 32. However, students are now operating with $1\frac{1}{8}$ of a mile instead of $\frac{1}{8}$ of a mile. The same strategies can be used here. For example, some students may prefer to use repeated addition: $2 \times 1\frac{1}{8} = 1\frac{1}{8} + 1\frac{1}{8}$.

**Planning** Students can work on problems **11** and **13** in pairs or in small groups. You may want to use problems **11** and **12** for individual assessment. Strategies should be compared in a class discussion.

**Comments about the Problems**

**11. Informal Assessment** This problem assesses students' ability to use informal strategies for operations with fractions. If students are having difficulty, they may use the drawing on Student Activity Sheet 12 and count the number of one-eighths of a mile. Encourage these students to find another strategy. Students may also "split" mixed fractions when multiplying. For example, to solve $10 \times 1\frac{1}{8}$, some students may first multiply $10 \times 1$ and then multiply $10 \times \frac{1}{8}$ and add the two products. Accept any notation if the answer is correct.

**12. Informal Assessment** This problem assesses students' ability to use equivalent forms of benchmark fractions and to order and compare fractions within a context. It may be helpful to refer students to the fraction strip activities if they are having difficulty with this problem.

**13. a.** Students can use their answers to problem **11** to complete the table.

**b.** Different strategies are possible. Some students may double the number of miles equal to four stretches and add the number of miles equal to two stretches. Others may first find the number of miles for five stretches and then double that distance. Still other students may notice the pattern in the table between the number of stretches and the number of miles to obtain an answer of $10\frac{10}{8}$ or $1\frac{10}{8}$ miles.

To raise money for the literacy group, the participants have to find people who will sponsor them. Meg, Mary, and Rodolfo each have pledges totaling $5.25 for each stretch they run.

**14.** How much money will each of them collect if they run all of their stretches?

**15.** Jami collected $21. How much did she get for each stretch?

Brenda is training for next year's Cedarberg–Poplarville race. She wants to use the Literacy Run as extra training, so she decides to run about 18 miles.

**16.** How many stretches does Brenda have to run?

**17.** Del wants to run about 8 miles. How many stretches should he plan to run?

**18.** How many stretches would it take to cover $13\frac{1}{8}$ miles?

## Solutions and Samples
*of student work*

**14.** Meg      $21.00

   Mary     $42.00

   Rodolfo  $31.50

**15.** $4.20

**16.** 16 stretches

**17.** about 7 stretches

**18.** $11\frac{2}{3}$ or about 12 stretches

**Overview** Within the same context, students solve more problems involving operations with fractions.

**About the Mathematics** Students further develop their understanding of and strategies for multiplying and dividing with fractions. The first two problems are related to problem **11**, but now students must work with the relationship that one stretch (the distance from Town Hall to the turnaround point) is equal to $5.25 in pledge money rather than the previous relationship of one stretch being equal to a distance of $1\frac{1}{8}$ miles. Problems **16** and **17** focus again on the relationship between the number of stretches and the corresponding total distance in miles.

**Planning** Students must use information from problem **11** to solve these problems. All the problems may be assigned as homework. You may use problems **14** and **15** for assessment. Students can work on problems **14–18** in pairs or in small groups.

**Comments about the Problems**

**14–15. Informal Assessment** These problems assess students' ability to use informal strategies for operations with fractions. Observe which strategies students use to solve the problems. Encourage them to use a ratio table to organize their calculations.

**16. Homework** This problem may be assigned for homework. Students may immediately see that Brenda runs twice as many stretches as Mary.

**17. Homework** This problem may be assigned for homework. Students can estimate the number of stretches using one of the following strategies:

- referring to the table from problem **11** to see that six stretches are $6\frac{3}{4}$ miles, and eight stretches are nine miles, so seven stretches will be about eight miles, or

- finding the number of miles equal to seven stretches by adding the number of miles equal to three and four stretches: $3\frac{3}{8}$ miles $+ 4\frac{1}{2}$ miles is about eight miles.

**18. Homework** This problem may be assigned as homework. Students may use different strategies. One strategy is to start with 10 stretches, or $11\frac{1}{4}$ miles, and then add the number of miles equal to two stretches in order to get close to $13\frac{1}{8}$ miles. A second strategy is to use information from problem **11.** Sixteen stretches is 18 miles (twice Mary's distance from problem **11**), and four stretches is $4\frac{1}{2}$ miles (Meg's distance from problem **11**); $18 - 4\frac{1}{2} = 13\frac{1}{2}$ miles, and $16 - 4 = 12$ stretches.

**Extension** After students have finished these problems, you may ask them to choose the number of stretches they would run if they were in a similar race. Have them convert the number of stretches into miles, or vice versa.

# Summary

Many different things can be divided into equal parts and named with fractions. When distances are measured, fractions can be used because a measurement unit can be divided into equal parts.

*Ratio tables* and *fraction strips* are tools that can be helpful when you work with fractions.

## Summary Questions

19. Ms. Cole's class decides to order a giant submarine sandwich for the end-of-the-year picnic. They wonder if one sandwich 78 inches long will serve all 25 people in the class. If a serving is $3\frac{3}{4}$ inches, will there be enough? How could you defend your answer to the class?

20. Another class decides that each person in the class should receive $3\frac{1}{3}$ inches of a giant submarine sandwich. If there are 24 people in the class, how long does the giant submarine sandwich need to be to serve them all?

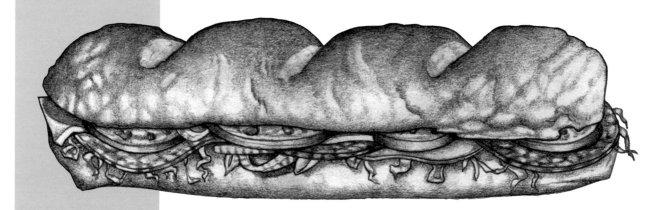

**19.** No, there will only be enough for between 20 and 21 people if you use $3\frac{3}{4}$-inch servings. Students' strategies will vary.

Sample strategy using a ratio table:

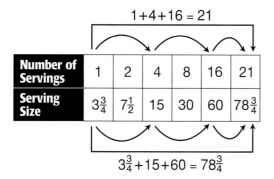

Since 78 inches is a little bit less than $78\frac{3}{4}$, the 78-inch sub would serve fewer than 21 people.

**20.** The sub needs to be 80 inches long. Students' strategies will vary.

Sample strategy using a ratio table:

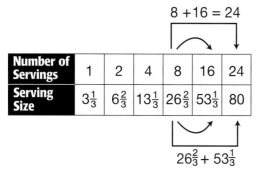

Sample strategy using multiplication computation:

$24 \times 3\frac{1}{3}$

I know that $24 \times 3 = 72$ inches. Each student still needs $\frac{1}{3}$ of an inch. There are three one-thirds in one inch, so $24\frac{1}{3}$ will make 8 more inches. So the sub needs to be 80 inches long.

**Overview** Students read the Summary and use fractions to solve problems involving the partitioning of a giant submarine sandwich.

**About the Mathematics** The Summary reviews the main math concepts of this unit:

- The number line is a useful tool to help students compare and order fractons.

- Distances given in a measurement unit, such as blocks or miles, can be subdivided into fractional parts.

- The double number line and ratio table models are useful tools to help students understand the relationship between any two measurement units, such as blocks and miles.

**Planning** Students can work on problems **19** and **20** individually or in pairs. You may decide to use these problems as assessments. After students complete Section E, you may assign appropriate activities in the Try This! section, located on pages 38–41 of the Student Book, for homework.

**Comments about the Problems**

**19–20. Informal Assessment** These problems assess students' ability to solve contextual problems in which fractions are involved, using informal strategies. Possible strategies include the following:

- drawing a picture and using a double number line strategy or a ratio table, or

- using different methods of repeated addition or subtraction.

These problems may provide an opportunity to discuss the relationship between multiplication and division and the use of a double number line or ratio table.

## Assessment Overview

Students work on five assessment activities that you can use to collect information about what each student knows about fractions and what strategies they use to solve each problem.

## Goals

- recognize part-whole relationships

- use fractions to describe part-whole relationships

- estimate fractions and parts of wholes

- use informal strategies for operations with fractions

- use equivalent forms of benchmark fractions within a context

- order and compare fractions within a context

- develop an understanding of and use the relationships between benchmark fractions

- understand the relative nature of fractions

- solve contextual problems in which simple fractions are involved, using informal strategies

## Assessment Opportunities

Remember When?
Bars of Different Sizes

Remember When?
Bars of Different Sizes

A Cycling Race

Bars of Different Sizes
Tropical Smoothie
A New Fence

Tropical Smoothie
A Cycling Race

Remember When?
Bars of Different Sizes
A Cycling Race

Remember When?
Tropical Smoothie
A Cycling Race

Bars of Different Sizes
A Cycling Race

Bars of Different Sizes
Tropical Smoothie
A Cycling Race
A New Fence

## Pacing

- Approximately one 45-minute class session for the three assessment activities, Bars of Different Sizes, Tropical Smoothie, and A New Fence. The other two assessment activities, Remember When and A Cycling Race, can be assigned as extra practice or homework.

## About the Mathematics

These five assessment activities assess the majority of the goals in the unit *Some of the Parts.* Refer to the Goals and Assessment Opportunities section on the facing page for information regarding the goals that are evaluated in each assessment activity. The activities do not ask students to use a specific strategy. Students have the option of using their own strategies or any of the strategies with which they feel comfortable. They may also choose any of the models that are introduced and developed in this unit (ratio table, bar model, or number line). Students are not expected to use any formal algorithms to solve these activities. They should demonstrate understanding and not mastery of the formal fraction concepts (adding, subtracting, and multiplying fractions; comparing and ordering fractions; estimating fractions; understanding the meaning of equivalent fractions; mixed numbers; and improper fractions).

## Materials

- Assessments, pages 115–119 of this Teacher Guide (one of each per student)
- fraction strips from Student Activity Sheet 3, page 105 of the Teacher Guide, optional (one set per student)

## Planning Assessment

Make sure that you allow enough time for students to complete the assessment activities. You may want students to work on these assessments individually or in pairs, depending on the nature of the class and your goals for assessment. Have fraction strips available for students who choose to use them.

## Scoring

The emphasis in scoring should be on the strategies used to solve the problems rather than on students' final answers. Since several strategies can be employed to answer many of the questions, the strategies that students choose may indicate how well they understand fraction concepts and problems. For example, a concrete strategy supported by drawings may indicate a deeper understanding than an abstract computation. Consider how well students' strategies address the problem, as well as how successful students are at applying their strategies in the problem-solving process.

# REMEMBER WHEN?

*Use additional paper as needed.*

In the first section, you solved this problem:

## Jake gets...?

Tim, Kelsey, Nick, Sandy, Dorothy, and Jules came up with these solutions.

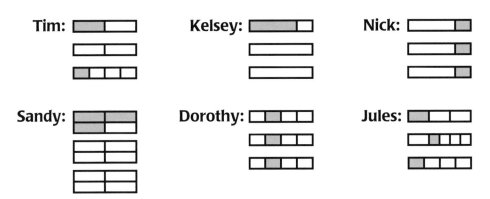

**1.** Which solutions are correct?

**2.** Explain, using fractions, how each person solved the problem.

## Solutions and Samples
*of student work*

1. All of the solutions are correct.

2. Tim $\quad\frac{1}{2} + \frac{1}{4}$

   Kelsey $\quad\frac{3}{4}$

   Nick $\quad\frac{1}{4} + \frac{1}{4} + \frac{1}{4}$

   or $3 \times \frac{1}{4}$

   Sandy $\quad\frac{1}{2} + \frac{1}{4}$

   or the same as Nick

   Dorothy $\quad 3 \times \frac{1}{4}$

   or $\frac{1}{4} + \frac{1}{4} + \frac{1}{4}$

   Jules $\quad\frac{1}{3} + \frac{1}{6} + \frac{1}{4}$

   or $\frac{1}{3} + \frac{1}{4}$ of $\frac{2}{3} + \frac{1}{4}$

   Sample written explanation:

   Jules divided the first sub into thirds. Since there were four people, they needed another third. So Jules marked one-third on the second sub. This left him with two-thirds of a sub. He divided the two-thirds into fourths, so that each piece was one-sixth of a whole sub. Finally, he divided the last sub into fourths.

## Hints and Comments

**Materials** Remember When? assessment, page 115 of the Teacher Guide (one per student)

**Overview** Students recognize, interpret, and name fractions.

**About the Mathematics** These activities assess students' ability to divide wholes into equal parts and label the parts using fractions. The activities also indicate student's knowledge of fraction equivalency.

Students may use different strategies to solve these problems:

- regrouping the shaded parts to get one-fourth of the total,

- drawing additional partitions on the bars in order to get parts of the same size to facilitate the counting of parts, or

- looking at the total of the three bars or looking at each bar separately and then dividing each bar into four equal pieces.

**Planning** You may want students to work individually on these assessment activities.

### Comments about the Problems

1. This problem assesses students' understanding of dividing wholes into equal parts by analyzing visual representations.

2. Students must label the parts with fractions. Some students may have done this already when answering problem **1.**

# BARS OF DIFFERENT SIZES

*Use additional paper as needed.*

Mahere was having a birthday party. She made two pans of brownies for her guests. The pans were the same size, but she cut the brownies in one pan into 16 pieces, while her mother cut those in the other pan into 24 pieces. They took brownies from each pan and put them on a platter for serving.

1. Two of Mahere's friends, Meagan and Ki, each had three brownies. Meagan told Ki that she did not eat as much as he did. Explain all the ways that this could be true.

1. Answers will vary. A brownie taken from the pan of 16 brownies is larger than a brownie taken from a pan of 24 brownies. Using that information, here are the ways the statement could be true:

   • Meagan: 3 small brownies,
     and Ki: 1 small brownie and 2 large brownies

   • Meagan: 3 small brownies,
     and Ki: 2 small brownies and 1 large brownie

   • Meagan: 3 small brownies,
     and Ki: 3 large brownies

   • Meagan: 2 small brownies and 1 large brownie,
     and Ki: 1 small brownie and 2 large brownies

   • Meagan: 2 small brownies and 1 large brownie,
     and Ki: 3 large brownies

   • Meagan: 1 small brownie and 2 large brownies,
     and Ki: 3 large brownies

**Materials** Bars of Different Sizes assessment, page 116 of the Teacher Guide (one per student)

**Overview** Students compare two distributions of a whole and make combinations of the parts (or fractions).

**About the Mathematics** These activities assess students' understanding of the relative nature of fractions. For example, when comparing the different-sized brownies in the two pans, students may realize that one-half of the brownies in the large pan is not equal to one-half of the brownies in the smaller pan. Students might use the fractions $\frac{1}{16}$ and $\frac{1}{24}$ to describe the different sizes of the brownies, although this is not necessary to answer the question. Students' reasoning about the relative sizes of the brownies may provide more insight into their understanding of this concept.

**Planning** You may want students to work individually on this assessment activity.

### Comments about the Problems

1. Students may draw the two different-sized brownies and visually show the possible combinations. The two extreme situations possible are: three large brownies or three small brownies. By exchanging a small brownie for a large one, the total amount in each combination changes. This method of reasoning may help students who are having difficulty.

# TROPICAL SMOOTHIE

*Use additional paper as needed.*

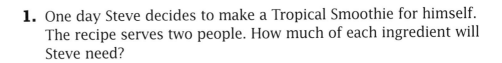

## Tropical Smoothie

*Serves two*

1 ripe banana
$\frac{1}{4}$ ripe cantaloupe
$\frac{1}{3}$ cup nonfat or low-fat frozen yogurt
2 Tbs skim milk powder
4 tsp pineapple-orange juice concentrate
2 tsp honey
$\frac{1}{2}$ tsp pure vanilla extract

Cut the banana into chunks and put in a blender or food processor. Seed the cantaloupe quarter and cut the flesh from the rind. Cut the flesh into chunks and add to the blender. Add the remaining ingredients and blend until smooth.

**1.** One day Steve decides to make a Tropical Smoothie for himself. The recipe serves two people. How much of each ingredient will Steve need?

**2.** Steve decides to call his friend Julio and invite him over for a Tropical Smoothie. Julio arrives at Steve's house with his friend Tim. Now how much of each ingredient will Steve need?

## Solutions and Samples
*of student work*

**1–2.** The correct ingredient amounts for one, two, and three servings are shown below. Students do not need to draw a ratio table to answer these problems.

| Servings | 2 | 1 | 3 |
|---|---|---|---|
| Bananas | 1 | $\frac{1}{2}$ | $1\frac{1}{2}$ |
| Cantaloupes | $\frac{1}{4}$ | $\frac{1}{8}$ | $\frac{3}{8}$ |
| Frozen Yogurt (cups) | $\frac{1}{3}$ | $\frac{1}{6}$ | $\frac{1}{2}$ |
| Skim Milk Powder (Tbs) | 2 | 1 | 3 |
| Pineapple-Orange Juice (tsp) | 4 | 2 | 6 |
| Honey (tsp) | 2 | 1 | 3 |
| Vanilla (tsp) | $\frac{1}{2}$ | $\frac{1}{4}$ | $\frac{3}{4}$ |

## Hints and Comments

**Materials** Tropical Smoothie assessment, page 117 of the Teacher Guide (one per student)

**Overview** Students use a recipe that yields two servings to determine the quantity of ingredients needed for one serving and three servings.

**About the Mathematics** Students may use a variety of strategies to solve these activities:
- making and using a ratio table,
- using fraction strips (or, a number line) to represent each ingredient,
- designing a measuring cup to find the correct quantities,
- doubling and halving the amounts of each ingredient.

**Planning** You may want students to work individually on these assessment activities.

### Comments about the Problems

1. To make one serving, the amount of each ingredient needs to be halved. Students may use a fraction strip, a ratio table, or another strategy.

2. If students use a ratio table, look for the operations they choose to create the column for three servings. One student may add the numbers in the first two columns, while another may multiply the numbers in the second column by three.

# A CYCLING RACE

*Use additional paper as needed.*

Sue, Maria, Ellen, Gloria, and Tracy are participating in a cycling race from Eldon to Durbridge. Without knowing the distance between Eldon and Durbridge, you should still be able to answer the following questions.

1. At a certain point in the race, Sue has cycled $\frac{1}{3}$ of the distance, and Maria has cycled $\frac{2}{5}$ of the distance. Who is ahead? (Hint: Make up a distance between Eldon and Durbridge.)

2. At another point in the race, Maria has cycled $\frac{4}{5}$ of the distance, and Ellen has cycled $\frac{3}{4}$ of the distance. Now which of the girls is ahead?

3. Toward the end of the race, the leaders are Gloria and Tracy. Gloria has cycled $\frac{5}{6}$ of the distance, and Tracy has cycled $\frac{7}{8}$ of the distance. If they both maintain their pace, who will win?

**1.** Maria is ahead. Explanations will vary.

Sample student explanations:

*Suppose the distance of the race is 15 kilometers. Sue has cycled $\frac{1}{3}$ of 15 kilometers, or 5 kilometers. Maria has cycled $\frac{2}{5}$ of 15 kilometers, or 6 kilometers. So Maria is ahead of Sue.*

Some students may make a drawing and reason with fractions:

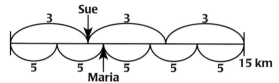

**2.** Maria is ahead. Explanations will vary.

Sample student explanations.

*Suppose the distance of the race is 20 kilometers. Maria has traveled $\frac{4}{5}$ of 20 kilometers, or 16 kilometers. Ellen has traveled $\frac{3}{4}$ of 20 kilometers, or 15 kilometers. So Maria is ahead of Ellen.*

Some students may make a drawing and reason with fractions:

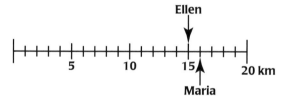

**3.** Tracy will win. Explanations will vary.

Sample student explanation:

*Suppose the distance of the race is 24 kilometers. Gloria has traveled $\frac{5}{6}$ of 24 kilometers, or 20 kilometers. Tracy has traveled $\frac{7}{8}$ of 24 kilometers, or 21 kilometers. So Tracy is ahead and will win the race.*

**Materials** A Cycling Race assessment, page 118 of the Teacher Guide (one per student)

**Overview** Students compare distances expressed in fractions without knowing the distance that represents the "whole."

**About the Mathematics** Students' understanding of the relative nature of fractions is assessed in these activities. Students can use any strategy to solve the problems. Some students may choose a number to represent the total distance to help them reason and to make it easier to compare the fractions. Others may use a number line to visualize the situation.

Students may also reason qualitatively by comparing the relative value of each fraction. For example, in problem **3** students may reason that $\frac{1}{6}$ is greater than $\frac{1}{8}$, so Tracy is closer to the finish line. Comparing fractions is easier when the fractions involved have a numerator of one or a numerator one less than the denominator (as in problems **2** and **3**).

**Planning** You may want students to work individually on these assessment activities.

**Comments about the Problems**

**1.** When comparing $\frac{1}{3}$ to $\frac{2}{5}$, students may think of a number that is divisible by both three and five to represent the whole distance. For example, using 30 kilometers as the total distance, $\frac{1}{3}$ of 30 = 10, and $\frac{2}{5}$ of 30 = 12. Students may also make a drawing to visualize the situation.

**2.** When comparing $\frac{4}{5}$ to $\frac{3}{4}$, students may choose a number divisible by both four and five, such as 20. If students divided their drawing for problem **1** into 15 equal sections, they cannot use the same partitions to solve this problem.

**3.** If students have used drawings with partitions of 15, 20, or 30 for problems **1** and **2,** they cannot use these divisions for problem **3.** Students may draw fraction bars (that are the same size) for $\frac{5}{6}$ and $\frac{7}{8}$ to compare their relative sizes.

# A NEW FENCE

*Use additional paper as needed.*

The school officials in Cedarberg want to build a fence around the school yard. The fence will be made of planks and posts. It is supposed to look like the drawing below.

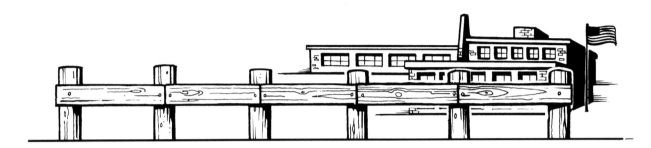

1. How long is a fence with 10 planks if each plank is 2 yards long? How many poles are needed?

The contractor has planks that are 2 yards and others that are $2\frac{3}{4}$ yards long.

2. How long is a fence that is made with 10 planks of $2\frac{3}{4}$ yards? How many poles are needed?

Suppose that the contractor wants to build a fence that is 22 yards long.

3. How many 2-yard planks and how many poles will be needed?

4. How many $2\frac{3}{4}$-yard planks and how many poles will be needed to build the same fence?

5. If you were building the 22-yard fence, would you use the 2-yard or $2\frac{3}{4}$-yard planks? Explain how you made your choice.

1. A new fence with 10 planks is 20 yards long, with 11 poles.

 Using a drawing:

2. The fence is $27\frac{1}{2}$ yards long, with 11 poles. Possible explanations:

 Ten times two equals 20, and 10 times $\frac{3}{4}$ equals $\frac{30}{4}$, which equals $7\frac{1}{2}$; $20 + 7\frac{1}{2} = 27\frac{1}{2}$ yards.

 The ratio table below uses doubling and addition.

 |                    | ×2 | ×2 | ×2 | +2 |
 |--------------------|----|----|----|----|
 | **Number of Planks** | 1 | 2 | 4 | 8 | 10 |
 | **Length (yds)** | $2\frac{3}{4}$ | $5\frac{1}{2}$ | 11 | 22 | $27\frac{1}{2}$ |

3. 11 planks and 12 poles

4. eight planks and nine poles

 Possible solution using a ratio table and doubling.

 |                    | ×2 | ×2 | ×2 |
 |--------------------|----|----|----|
 | **Number of Planks** | 1 | 2 | 4 | 8 |
 | **Length (yds)** | $2\frac{3}{4}$ | $5\frac{1}{2}$ | 11 | 22 |

 Possible solution by splitting $2\frac{3}{4}$ into 2 and $\frac{3}{4}$, and then adding the results.

 | **Number of Planks** | 1 | 2 | 4 | 8 |
 |--------------------|----|----|----|----|
 | **Length (yds)** | 2 | 4 | 8 | 16 |

 | **Number of Planks** | 1 | 2 | 4 | 8 |
 |--------------------|----|----|----|----|
 | **Length (yds)** | $\frac{3}{4}$ | $1\frac{1}{2}$ | 3 | 6 |

 16 yds + 6 yds = 22 yds

5. Answers will vary. Either choice is acceptable. Sample response:

 If you use 2-yard planks, you need more poles. If you use $2\frac{3}{4}$-yard planks, you need fewer poles, but the fence may be weaker.

---

**Materials** A New Fence assessment, page 119 of the Teacher Guide (one per student)

**Overview** Given different numbers of poles and planks, students determine the lengths of different fences. They also find the number of poles and planks needed to build a fence that is 22 yards long.

**About the Mathematics** In Problem **2**, students may use informal methods to multiply with mixed numbers, such as splitting the mixed number $2\frac{3}{4}$ and multiplying in two steps:
$10 \times 2\frac{3}{4} =$
$(10 \times 2) + (10 \times \frac{3}{4}) =$
$20 + 7\frac{1}{2} = 27\frac{1}{2}$

The number line is not the most efficient strategy here, although it can be used. A ratio table can also be used to record the fence lengths for different numbers of planks.

**Planning** You may want students to work individually on these assessment activities.

**Comments about the Problems**

 1. Most students will easily compute the length of the fence by multiplying 10 by two. Some students may not realize that the total number of poles needed is one more than the total number of planks. A drawing may make this clear.

 2. This problem can be more easily computed by splitting $2\frac{3}{4}$ into 2 and $\frac{3}{4}$. Students can multiply $10 \times 2$ and $10 \times \frac{3}{4}$ and add the two results. Because the total number of planks is the same as in problem **1,** the number of poles is also the same.

 3. This is a division problem, and the total number of poles is, again, one more than the total number of planks.

 4. Students can start with one plank, double its length to find the length of two planks, double again to find the length for four planks, and so on until they reach a length of 22 yards. They may also split the length of a plank into 2 yards plus $\frac{3}{4}$ yards to more easily compute the answer.

 5. Students must think back to problems **3** and **4** (and their solutions) and think realistically about fence construction.

---

## *Some of the Parts*
# Glossary

The Glossary defines all vocabulary words listed on the Section Opener pages. It includes the mathematical terms that may be new to students, as well as words having to do with the contexts introduced in the unit. (Note: The Student Book has no glossary in order to allow students to construct their own definitions, based on their personal experiences with the unit activities.)

The definitions below are specific to the use of the terms in this unit. The page numbers given are from this Teacher Guide.

**deciliter** (p. 48) a measure for volume; there are 10 deciliters in one liter and 10 milliliters in one deciliter

**denominator** (p. 22) the part of a fraction that is below the line and that represents the total number of parts into which a unit is divided

**equivalent fraction** (p. 18) fractions that name the same number; $\frac{1}{2}$ and $\frac{2}{4}$ are equivalent fractions

**fraction** (p. 8) a numerical representation of numerator over denominator, such as $\frac{1}{2}$ or $\frac{3}{5}$, that represents the division of one number by another

**fraction bar** (p. 54) a visual model used to show the part-whole relationship of fractions; a rectangular-shaped bar that is divided into so many equal parts. The top of the bar is labeled to show a range from zero to a certain quantity. The bottom of the bar is labeled to show the corresponding fractional parts.

**fraction strip** (p. 4) rectangular strips of paper of equal lengths that are divided into equal-sized parts; for example, a fraction strip showing fourths is divided into four equal parts with each part labeled *one-fourth*

**improper fraction** (p. 18) fractions in which the number in the numerator is larger than the number in the denominator; $\frac{10}{4}$ is an improper fraction

**liter** (p. 48) a measure for volume; there are 10 deciliters or 1,000 milliliters in one liter

**mixed number** (p. 30) a number composed of an integer and a fraction; $1\frac{1}{2}$ is a mixed number

**numerator** (p. 22) the part of a fraction that is above the line and that represents "so many parts" of the denominator

**part-whole relationship** (p. 4) the relationship between the numerator and denominator of a fraction; the numerator represents "so many parts" of the denominator which represents the "whole"

**ratio table** (p. 44) a table in which each column presents numbers that have the same ratio as numbers in other columns (see example below)

| 1 | 2 | 10 | 20 |
|---|---|----|----|
| 5 | 10 | 50 | 100 |

**volume** (p. 36) the amount of space inside a three-dimensional figure

# Blackline Masters

# Letter to the Family

## Dear Family,

Your child is about to begin working on the *Mathematics in Context* unit *Some of the Parts*. Below is a letter to your child describing the unit and its goals.

You can help your child relate the class work to his or her own life by talking about fractions as you encounter them in recipes ($\frac{1}{4}$ cup of sugar), retail sales (all items are $\frac{1}{2}$ price), butcher shops ($1\frac{3}{4}$ pounds of hamburger), and so on.

Ask your child to show you what $\frac{1}{3}$ of a glass of milk looks like. Then ask to see $\frac{3}{4}$ of a glass of milk. See if your child can determine, without pouring, whether or not the two fractions together would exceed one full glass. Then check his or her answer by combining the portions.

You might also ask your child to extend a recipe to serve twice as many people. He or she would then have to decide, for instance, what $2 \times \frac{1}{4}$ teaspoon of salt is.

Encourage your child to think about and discuss fractions. Enjoy investigating fractions with your child.

### Dear Student,

Welcome to *Some of the Parts*.

In this unit, you will learn how the parts of quantities and objects we call fractions relate to the whole.

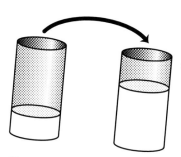

You will use fractions to measure and combine quantities of milk. Will $\frac{1}{3}$ of a can of milk and $\frac{5}{8}$ of a can of milk fit into one can?

Knowing about relationships between fractions will help you alter recipes to serve different numbers of people.

You will also learn how fractions can help you measure and calculate distances.

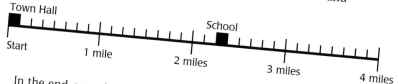

In the end, you should understand something about relationships between fractions. You will also use your understanding of fractions to add, subtract, multiply, and divide with them.

Sincerely,

*The Mathematics in Context Development Team*

Sincerely,

*The Mathematics in Context Development Team*

**Emmy gets…?**

**Jake gets…?**

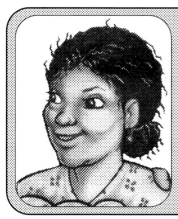

**Sandra gets…?**

**Walter gets…?**

Name_____

Use with *Some of the Parts*, page 3.

**5.** Below are six pieces of fruit tape. Cut them out.

Divide and cut each fruit tape into the number of pieces indicated on **Student Activity Sheet 3.** Be sure that your pieces are equal. Glue the pieces onto the bars on **Student Activity Sheet 3.** Label each piece with a fraction. Be prepared to explain how you decided where to cut.

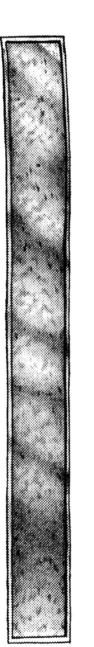
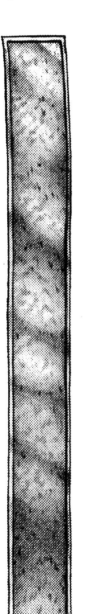
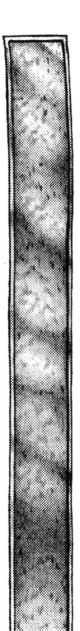

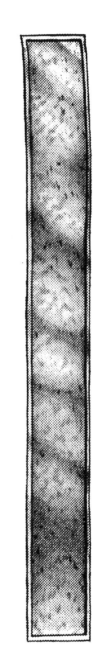
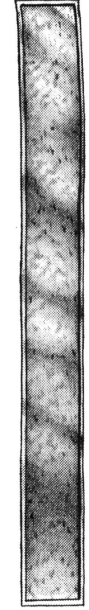

**Name**_____

| 2 equal pieces | 4 equal pieces | 8 equal pieces | 3 equal pieces | 6 equal pieces | 5 equal pieces |
|---|---|---|---|---|---|
|  |  |  |  |  |  |

Name_____

Use with *Some of the Parts*, page 9.

$\frac{3}{4}$ can

$\frac{5}{8}$ can

$\frac{1}{3}$ can

$\frac{4}{6}$ can

$\frac{1}{2}$

$\frac{2}{3}$ $\frac{1}{3}$

$\frac{3}{4}$ $\frac{2}{4}$ $\frac{1}{4}$

$\frac{4}{5}$ $\frac{3}{5}$ $\frac{2}{5}$ $\frac{1}{5}$

$\frac{5}{6}$ $\frac{4}{6}$ $\frac{3}{6}$ $\frac{2}{6}$ $\frac{1}{6}$

$\frac{7}{8}$ $\frac{6}{8}$ $\frac{5}{8}$ $\frac{4}{8}$ $\frac{3}{8}$ $\frac{2}{8}$ $\frac{1}{8}$

$\frac{8}{9}$ $\frac{7}{9}$ $\frac{6}{9}$ $\frac{5}{9}$ $\frac{4}{9}$ $\frac{3}{9}$ $\frac{2}{9}$ $\frac{1}{9}$

$\frac{9}{10}$ $\frac{8}{10}$ $\frac{7}{10}$ $\frac{6}{10}$ $\frac{5}{10}$ $\frac{4}{10}$ $\frac{3}{10}$ $\frac{2}{10}$ $\frac{1}{10}$

$\frac{11}{12}$ $\frac{10}{12}$ $\frac{9}{12}$ $\frac{8}{12}$ $\frac{7}{12}$ $\frac{6}{12}$ $\frac{5}{12}$ $\frac{4}{12}$ $\frac{3}{12}$ $\frac{2}{12}$ $\frac{1}{12}$

## Student Activity Sheet 6

Name_____

Use with *Some of the Parts*, page 18.

**7.** Complete the table below so that Juan and his friends can make 24 pizza patterns.

| | | | | |
|---|---|---|---|---|
| **Number of Pizzas** | 4 | | | |
| **Cups of Bread Crumbs** | $\frac{1}{3}$ | | | |
| **Jars of Spaghetti Sauce** | 1 | | | |
| **Pounds of Ground Beef** | 1 | | | |
| **Teaspoons of Dried Oregano** | $\frac{1}{2}$ | | | |
| **Number of Olives** | 2 | | | |
| **Cups of Shredded Mozzarella Cheese** | $\frac{1}{4}$ | | | |
| **Cups of Shredded Cheddar Cheese** | $\frac{1}{4}$ | | | |
| **Number of Mushrooms** | 4 | | | |

Name_____

**8.** Complete the table below for the Yogurt Cups recipe.

| Servings | 4 | 2 | 8 | 6 | 10 | 16 |
|---|---|---|---|---|---|---|
| Flour (cups) | $\frac{3}{4}$ | | | | | |
| Margarine (cups) | $\frac{1}{4}$ | | | | | |
| Powdered Sugar (tablespoons) | 3 | | | | | |
| Water (teaspoons) | $2\frac{1}{2}$ | | | | | |
| Yogurt (cups) | $1\frac{1}{3}$ | | | | | |

Name_____

Use with *Some of the Parts*, page 21.

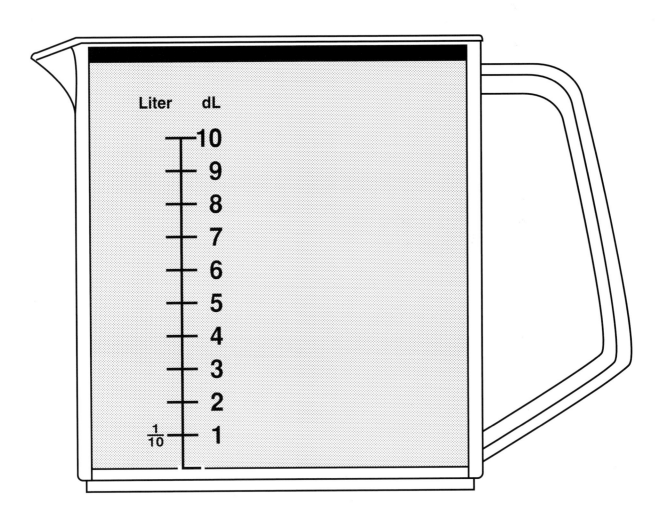

**14. b.** Write the fractions of a liter that correspond to the measuring lines pictured above.

**15.** Draw measuring lines for $\frac{1}{3}$ liter and $\frac{2}{3}$ liter on the measuring cup.

**16.** How many deciliters are in $\frac{1}{3}$ liter?

1. Use the table below to decide how much of each ingredient Eileen and her mother will need to make the recipe for only four servings.

| | | |
|---|---|---|
| **Number of Servings** | 8 | |
| **Number of Chicken Breast Halves** | 8 | |
| **Jars of Salsa** | 1 | |
| **Cups of Light Sour Cream** | 1 | |
| **Cups of Half-and-Half** | $\frac{1}{2}$ | |
| **Number of Corn Tortillas** | 12 | |
| **Cups of Shredded Cheddar Cheese** | 4 | |
| **Cups of Grated Parmesan Cheese** | $\frac{1}{3}$ | |

Name_____

Use with *Some of the Parts,* page 25.

**3.** Draw lines and color the piece on each food item that is needed by the cafeteria staff.

**a.** This piece of bologna weighs 400 grams. Cut off 100 grams.

**b.** This piece of salami weighs 600 grams. Cut off 450 grams.

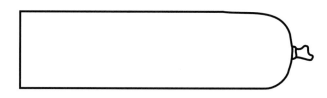

**c.** This piece of cheese weighs 1,200 grams. Cut off 800 grams.

**d.** This piece of cheese weighs 1,600 grams. Cut off 1,200 grams.

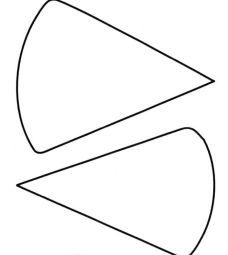

**e.** This piece of sausage weighs 1,200 grams. Cut off 200 grams.

**f.** This piece of sausage weighs 900 grams. Cut off 100 grams.

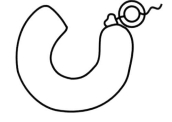

**g.** This piece of pepperoni weighs 2,400 grams. Cut off 2,000 grams.

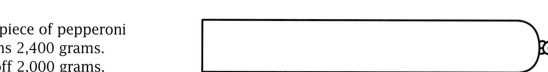

**2.** Complete the map below for the students by showing where the water stations will be.

# Student Activity Sheet 12

Name_____

Use with *Some of the Parts*, pages 32–34.

**5.** Locate on the city map where Belinda and Sylvia could live.

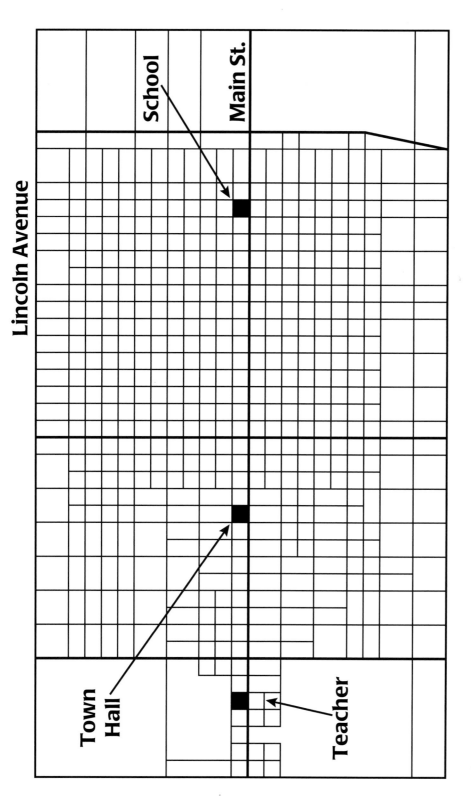

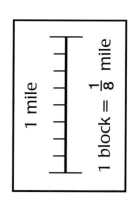

**10.** Mark the turnaround point for the run.

# REMEMBER WHEN?

*Use additional paper as needed.*

In the first section, you solved this problem:

**Jake gets...?**

Tim, Kelsey, Nick, Sandy, Dorothy, and Jules came up with these solutions.

**Tim:**  **Kelsey:**  **Nick:**

**Sandy:**  **Dorothy:**  **Jules:**

**1.** Which solutions are correct?

**2.** Explain, using fractions, how each person solved the problem.

# BARS OF DIFFERENT SIZES

*Use additional paper as needed.*

Mahere was having a birthday party. She made two pans of brownies for her guests. The pans were the same size, but she cut the brownies in one pan into 16 pieces, while her mother cut those in the other pan into 24 pieces. They took brownies from each pan and put them on a platter for serving.

1. Two of Mahere's friends, Meagan and Ki, each had three brownies. Meagan told Ki that she did not eat as much as he did. Explain all the ways that this could be true.

# TROPICAL SMOOTHIE

*Use additional paper as needed.*

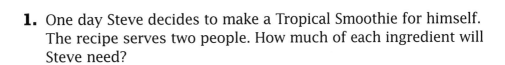

## Tropical Smoothie

*Serves two*

1 ripe banana
$\frac{1}{4}$ ripe cantaloupe
$\frac{1}{3}$ cup nonfat or low-fat frozen yogurt
2 Tbs skim milk powder
4 tsp pineapple-orange juice concentrate
2 tsp honey
$\frac{1}{2}$ tsp pure vanilla extract

Cut the banana into chunks and put in a blender or food processor. Seed the cantaloupe quarter and cut the flesh from the rind. Cut the flesh into chunks and add to the blender. Add the remaining ingredients and blend until smooth.

**1.** One day Steve decides to make a Tropical Smoothie for himself. The recipe serves two people. How much of each ingredient will Steve need?

**2.** Steve decides to call his friend Julio and invite him over for a Tropical Smoothie. Julio arrives at Steve's house with his friend Tim. Now how much of each ingredient will Steve need?

# A CYCLING RACE

*Use additional paper as needed.*

Sue, Maria, Ellen, Gloria, and Tracy are participating in a cycling race from Eldon to Durbridge. Without knowing the distance between Eldon and Durbridge, you should still be able to answer the following questions.

1. At a certain point in the race, Sue has cycled $\frac{1}{3}$ of the distance, and Maria has cycled $\frac{2}{5}$ of the distance. Who is ahead? (Hint: Make up a distance between Eldon and Durbridge.)

2. At another point in the race, Maria has cycled $\frac{4}{5}$ of the distance, and Ellen has cycled $\frac{3}{4}$ of the distance. Now which of the girls is ahead?

3. Towards the end of the race, the leaders are Gloria and Tracy. Gloria has cycled $\frac{5}{6}$ of the distance, and Tracy has cycled $\frac{7}{8}$ of the distance. If they both maintain their pace, who will win?

## A NEW FENCE

*Use additional paper as needed.*

The school officials in Cedarberg want to build a fence around the school yard. The fence will be made of planks and posts. It is supposed to look like the drawing below.

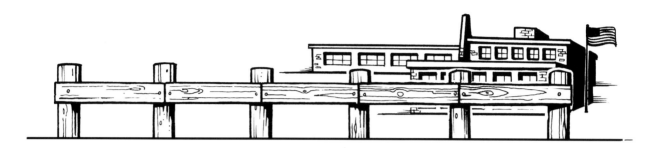

**1.** How long is a fence with 10 planks if each plank is 2 yards long? How many poles are needed?

The contractor has planks that are 2 yards and others that are $2\frac{3}{4}$ yards long.

**2.** How long is a fence that is made with 10 planks of $2\frac{3}{4}$ yards? How many poles are needed?

Suppose that the contractor wants to build a fence that is 22 yards long.

**3.** How many 2-yard planks and how many poles will be needed?

**4.** How many $2\frac{3}{4}$-yard planks and how many poles will be needed to build the same fence?

**5.** If you were building the 22-yard fence, would you use the 2-yard or $2\frac{3}{4}$-yard planks? Explain how you made your choice.

## Section A. Sharing Food

**1.** Drawings and descriptions will vary.

**2.** Each person will get $\frac{2}{3}$ of a sandwich.

**3.**

## Section B. Measure Up

**1.** Answers will vary. Sample response:

The denominator (8) represents the total number of equal parts into which the whole is divided. The numerator (5) represents the number of equal parts that make up the portion of the whole (such as the shaded part).

**2.** Yes. Explanations will vary. Sample explanation:

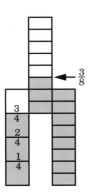

If you use the fraction strips, you can see that when you place the $\frac{3}{8}$ on top of the $\frac{3}{4}$, this makes a whole strip plus $\frac{1}{8}$ left over.

**3. a.** $\frac{9}{10}$ can

**b.** $\frac{11}{12}$ can

**4.** Answers will vary. Sample answer:

$\frac{1}{2}$ can + $\frac{1}{3}$ can

## Section C. Fractions and Recipes

**1. a.** Answers will vary. Sample answer:

Jovita can double the amount of oregano needed for four pizzas twice to determine how much is needed for 16 pizzas.

| Servings | 4 | 16 | 24 |
|---|---|---|---|
| Teaspoons | $\frac{1}{4}$ | 1 | $1\frac{1}{2}$ |

**b.** $1\frac{1}{2}$ teaspoons

**2.** Table entries will vary. Sample table:

| Pancakes | 6 | 12 | 18 |
|---|---|---|---|
| Mix (cups) | 1 | 2 | 3 |
| Water (cups) | $\frac{3}{4}$ | $1\frac{1}{2}$ | $2\frac{1}{4}$ |
| Eggs | 2 | 4 | 6 |
| Oil (cups) | $\frac{1}{4}$ | $\frac{1}{2}$ | $\frac{3}{4}$ |

Each person will receive $2\frac{1}{4}$ pancakes.

**3. a.** Multiply the numbers in the first column by three.

**b.** Answers will vary. Sample answer:

Multiply the numbers in column 2 by three to get the numbers in column 3.

## Section D. How Much?

**1.**

$\left(\frac{3}{4}\right)$

**2.** 484 grams $\left(\frac{2}{3}\right)$

## Section E.  How Far?

1. **a.** 2 miles

   **b.** the Fitness Center

   **c.** 36 blocks

   **d.** 48 blocks

2. $25\frac{1}{2}$ inches long

# CREDITS

## Cover

Design by Ralph Paquet/Encyclopædia Britannica Educational Corporation.

Collage by Koorosh Jamalpur/KJ Graphics.

## Title Page

Illustration by Paul Tucker/Encyclopædia Britannica Educational Corporation.

## Illustrations

**3, 6, 8, 10** Paul Tucker/Encyclopædia Britannica Educational Corporation; **12 (bottom)** Phil Geib/ Encyclopædia Britannica Educational Corporation; **12 (top), 14** Brent Cardillo/Encyclopædia Britannica Educational Corporation; **16** Paul Tucker/Encyclopædia Britannica Educational Corporation; **20** Jerome Gordon; **22, 24** Phil Geib/Encyclopædia Britannica Educational Corporation; **26, 30** Jerome Gordon; **32** Phil Geib/Encyclopædia Britannica Educational Corporation; **34** Paul Tucker/Encyclopædia Britannica Educational Corporation; **38, 40, 42, 44, 46, 56, 58, 60, 62, 64, 68, 74, 75, 76, 78** Phil Geib/Encyclopædia Britannica Educational Corporation; **82** Jerome Gordon; **84** Brent Cardillo/ Encyclopædia Britannica Educational Corporation; **86** Paul Tucker/Encyclopædia Britannica Educational Corporation; **90** Paul Tucker/Encyclopædia Britannica Educational Corporation; **92, 94, 96, 98,** Phil Geib/ Encyclopædia Britannica Educational Corporation; **102, 103** Paul Tucker/Encyclopædia Britannica Educational Corporation; **113** Phil Geib/Encyclopædia Britannica Educational Corporation; **115** Paul Tucker/Encyclopædia Britannica Educational Corporation; **116–119** Phil Geib/Encyclopædia Britannica Educational Corporation; **120** Paul Tucker/Encyclopædia Britannica Educational Corporation.

## Photographs

**80** © David Alexovich/Encyclopædia Britannica Educational Corporation.

*Mathematics in Context* is a registered trademark of Encyclopædia Britannica Educational Corporation. Other trademarks are registered trademarks of their respective owners.